6 FIGURES IN 12 MONTHS

6 FIGURES IN 12 MONTHS

HOW TO MEET OR SURPASS YOUR REVENUE GOALS AS A REAL ESTATE AGENT

JEFF DISCHER
BROKER | GRI | ABR | CNE | SFR | SRES | ePRO

BMcTALKS Press
4980 South Alma School Road
Suite 2-493
Chandler, Arizona 85248

Copyright © 2021 by Jeff Discher. All rights reserved.

No part of this publication may be reproduced in any form beyond the copying permitted by US Copyright Law, Section 107, "fair use" in teaching or research, Section 108, certain library copying, or in published media by reviewers in limited excerpts; stored in a retrieval system; or transmitted in any form or by any means, electronic, mechanical, photocopying, recording, scanning, or otherwise without the prior written permission of the Publisher. Requests to the Publisher for permissions should be submitted to the BMcTALKS Press, 4980 S. Alma School Road, Ste 2-493, Chandler, AZ 85248 or at www.bmctalkspress.com/permissions

Disclaimer: This book is for educational purposes only. The views expressed are those of the author alone and should not be taken as expert instruction or commands. The reader is responsible for his or her own actions. Adherence to all applicable laws and regulations, including international, federal, state, and local governing professional licensing, business practices, advertising, and all other aspects of doing business in the United States, Canada, or any other jurisdiction is the sole responsibility of the purchaser or reader. Neither the author nor the publisher assumes any responsibility or liability whatsoever on the behalf of the purchaser or reader of these materials.

The views expressed in this publication are those of the author; are the responsibility of the author; and do not necessarily reflect or represent the views of BMcTALKS Press, its owner, or its contractors.

Volume pricing is available to bulk orders placed by corporations, associations, and others. For details, please contact BMcTALKS Press at info@bmtpress.com

FIRST EDITION

Library of Congress Control Number: 2021911651

Hardcover: 978-1-953315-10-6
eBook: 978-1-953315-11-3

Cover and interior design by Medlar Publishing Solutions Pvt Ltd., India.

Photographer: Pat Schneider; IG: patcanfilmit

Printed in the United States of America.

DEDICATION

To
my mother for always believing in me
and being my biggest fan no matter what

ACKNOWLEDGMENTS

Ben Biggs for being so persistent with me to start a team

My mentors over the years: Kent Vegdahl, Mike Schiralli, Ken Pecus, Ashley Lunn, Ron Oster, Thomas Bell, and all my online mentors who don't even know they are mentoring me

My team for allowing me to coach them to their first six figures by listening to my coaching and believing in me enough to stick with it

CONTENTS

A Note from the Author — *Why You Should Listen to Me* . . . xi

Introduction — *Got Your License, Now What?* 1

READY YOUR MIND

CHAPTER 1
Morning Ritual — *Set Up Your Day to WIN!* 33

CHAPTER 2
Discipline and Habits — *Show Me Your Habits,
and I'll Show You Your Future* 59

CHAPTER 3
Personal Development and Growth — *Improve Every Day
in Every Way* 77

CHAPTER 4
Time Management and Time Blocking — *That Which
Gets Measured Gets Done* 89

BUILD STRONG BUSINESS FOUNDATIONS

CHAPTER 5
Focus Points of Business — *Go All-In on Three Activities* . . . 107

CHAPTER 6
Social Media — *Creative, Entertaining, Value-Focused* 115

CHAPTER 7
Open Houses — *Let Clients Come to You* 135

CHAPTER 8
Database — *Stay in Front of the People Who Know You* 145

INVEST IN YOUR BUSINESS

CHAPTER 9
Success Tools — *What it Takes to Run Your Business Successfully* 161

CHAPTER 10
Build Lasting Relationships — *Create Clients for Life* 175

CHAPTER 11
Business Planning — *If You Fail to Plan, You Plan to Fail* . . . 191

CHAPTER 12
Your Vendor Team — *Choose Your Team Wisely* 195

CONCLUSION
Your Next Move as a Real Estate Agent — *Join a Team or Work Solo?* 205

CONTENTS

APPENDICES

Appendix A: Stages of a Successful Career 215

Appendix B: Write Down Your Goals 218

Appendix C: Readers Are Leaders 220

Appendix D: Habits Can Be Good or Bad 224

Appendix E: Designations Help You Prove Your Value . . . 227

Appendix F: Manage Your Week to Win the Year 229

Appendix G: Leverage Accountability to Become
Successful Faster 232

Appendix H: Using the DiSC Assessment
to Up-level Your Business 234

Appendix I: Host a Six-Figure Open House 236

Appendix J: Creating Your Business Plan 241

About the Author 243

"If you want someone to be your mentor, you better be ready to listen and be humble."

– MAGIC JOHNSON

A NOTE FROM THE AUTHOR

Why You Should Listen to Me

I wrote this book as a simple guide for the real estate agent who wants to level up their business. I wanted to give a simple blueprint to remove some of the confusion for newer agents and for current agents who want to become successful in real estate as soon as possible. This is not a step-by-step guide detailing each and every step; it's more a guide to the lifestyle of a successful real estate agent with a great business.

Real estate is a way of life more than a career. At its core, it is about living, and you get to create those livable moments for your clients. It consumes you, and you must give into that obsession to surpass six figures in your next twelve months.

It's not just about real estate either; it's also about becoming the best version of yourself in the process. If you want to be a top-performing real estate agent, you must become that person in real life. Act as if you are *already* a top-performing agent. Read the books that person would read; be as healthy as that type of agent would need to be to have the energy needed to keep up with that level of success.

I'm talking about an intentional lifestyle. The good life. The life you design. Full responsibility for yourself, your actions, and your successes. I've explained everything in the simplest form possible, so no matter where you are in life, you should be able to digest this material and apply it immediately. Use this book as a tool to level up not only at the start of your career but whenever you need to get back on track.

I've trained multiple Rookie of the Years within several real estate brokerages. I know what works in real estate and what doesn't. I've taken multiple agents from zero to $100,000 in their first twelve months of being licensed. **It's simple, just not easy.** The quicker you can implement what you see in this book, the faster you will get the results.

I am giving you everything I give to my agents who go on to earn $100,000 or more in their first year. Everything and then some of what I used to earn a six-figure income since my first year of selling real estate. It works. If you don't believe me, you can direct message (DM) my agents on Facebook or Instagram and ask them yourself. They're waiting. Better yet, come down to the office and see how we get things done. We love guests. Be ready to have some fun and learn something new.

See you soon,
Jeff Discher, Broker | GRI | ABR | CNE | SFR | SRES | ePRO

INTRODUCTION

Got Your License, Now What?

You're freshly licensed, and you want to start your successful real estate career. You've passed your test, bought some new clothes, joined a brokerage, gotten your business cards, washed your car, and now what? Make a shit ton of money while going to happy hours; fine dining at the trending restaurants; attending real estate caravans with your friends; and sell huge, beautiful estates for millions of dollars while having more free time than you've ever had. We've seen it on TV, and we all know that one friend-of-a-friend who crushes it. They drive the brand-new BMW or Mercedes and always post pics of themselves on vacation, living the life you've always wanted, selling the beautiful homes and condos while having total freedom—or so it appears. Let's be real; that can be your life. Unfortunately, that dream existence is reserved for the top 5 to 10 percent of all real estate agents, and for a reason.

Real estate is like any other profession. Typically, it's the Pareto Principle of 80/20, meaning 20 percent of the realtors make 80 percent of the money. In real estate, it's more like the 90/10; 10 percent of the real estate agents make 90 percent of the money.

"Take the first step in faith. You don't have to see the whole staircase, just take the first step."

— MARTIN LUTHER KING, JR.

INTRODUCTION

I know attorneys, doctors, business owners, athletes, and many other professionals at both ends of the income scale, and these rules are applicable across the board.

Ever since I could remember, I wanted to know how super successful people got to that position and what separated them from the average. How did they become the best? How did Kobe Bryant become Kobe? How did Elon Musk become Elon Musk? How did Oprah become Oprah?

We want to believe they were born with it or were just lucky. We want to believe that they have something we don't. They grew up with more opportunity, with a better environment. 'There are so many factors that play into becoming successful. Some we can't control, most we can.

Where does it start? It starts with your childhood and parents. How did they live? How did they live before having you? The first seven years of your life were extremely important in your development and growth. Ultimately affecting your future self. Here's the quick version. The first seven years of your life, you are living in Theta State. This is when you learn the easiest and the fastest. Your brain and mind act as a sponge. Starting at age eight, you only experience that easy and fast state of learning twice a day. Once in the morning, while coming out of sleep into awareness, or unconscious to conscious, and the second time is when we go from awake to asleep. We'll go into those two times later. Let's go back to those first seven years.

Studies show that we are told "no" up to 400 times per day, even as babies. Without knowing, our parents are programming our subconscious minds to be in a negative state, and this can be psychologically damaging to a child. This sticks with us as we age and affects our lives without us even realizing it. The reason I bring this up is that those children that are told a form of "yes" instead of "no" tend to live their lives from a positive state. This is so important because these situations build and develop our self-confidence. As we get older, those who grow up in a more positive state will more often believe we "can" instead of we "can't." Children that grow up in a positive household are more likely to have more confidence than others.

So, can children that grow up in a negative household go on to be great? The answer is yes. Believe it or not, most of the most successful people in the world have had to overcome major adversity. I happen to be one of them. Tom Stanley, author of *The Millionaire Next Door*, found that about 20 percent of millionaires became millionaires through inheritance; the other 80 percent started from poverty.

OVERCOMING ADVERSITY

My level of success now may surprise you when you consider my background. At the time of this writing, I am forty-two years old. I grew up in a small area of San Diego called San Ysidro with a mother who was married five times and who had four children with three different husbands with her longest marriage lasting five years. I grew up in a trailer park, but she was never home because she was always at work to make ends meet, pay the rent, and put minimal food on the table.

From the age of five through the time I was in high school, I took care of myself. My two older brothers were in and out of prison from as young as the age of eleven, and my younger sister typically stayed with our neighbors. I was alone a lot or out with my friends, and my only male role models were my brothers.

I remember the conversations I had with my mother were minimal. She would always come home from work at night and bring me a piece of candy or sweets. She would then make a quick dinner or order a pizza. I ate so much pizza growing up that I can barely eat it now, but I don't blame her. We were broke, and she could

"Start by doing what's necessary; then do what is possible; and suddenly you are doing the impossible."

– FRANCIS OF ASSISI

feed her family of five for ten dollars. In retrospect, my mother was my subconscious role model. She was amazing in so many ways. She raised four kids by herself, worked a full-time job as a nursing assistant, and attended school at night to become a registered nurse. I remember seeing her cry because she couldn't figure out her schoolwork, and she would call my Uncle Gordon for help. Eventually, she did graduate from nursing school and went on to become a registered nurse. When she got her first job with her new title, we thought we were rich. She went from eight dollars an hour to fifteen dollars an hour. Life got a little better; however, we still had a poor mindset and were broke financially.

My father was gone before I can remember. My mom and brothers would tell me about how successful and rich he was all the time. My mother would always tell me, "You're so smart—just like your father." I didn't know it then, but as I got older, I realized that my mother was programming my subconscious to help me succeed later in life.

When I was twelve years old, I got my first paper route. You had to be twelve to get one, and it's all I wanted for my birthday was a job and to deliver newspapers. I would run home from seventh grade to my porch stacked with sections of newspaper that I had to assemble. Once they were all put together, I would load up my bike, put another stack on my shoulders, and off I went. I would pass by the front of my school and hear kids saying, "Is that Jeff Discher?" It was actually really embarrassing, but it was all worth it because every month, I would have money in my pocket. I got paid after collecting the monthly subscription payments from my customers and would stop by Circle K to buy Beckett Baseball Card Price Guides and *Muscle & Fitness* magazines. Those were my two obsessions: baseball cards and muscle magazines. I wanted to have muscles like the dudes in the magazines. I tell you this part of my

INTRODUCTION

life because that's when I started my entrepreneurial journey without even knowing it.

I realized that I liked to work because it gave me the freedom to buy and do what I wanted without anyone telling me "No." It was a great freedom that I loved. I went on to deliver newspapers for a few years until a drive-by occurred on my street; the neighbor was shot and killed right in front of my bedroom window. My mother freaked out and moved us as far east as she could while staying in San Diego County. She actually moved our trailer out to a piece of land that she and my brother's wife at the time had purchased together. It was six acres out in the middle of nowhere known as good old Campo, California. What my mother didn't know was it was worse out there than it was where we had been living.

I started eleventh grade out there and picked up the largest newspaper route in the area. I was in charge of delivering hundreds of newspapers every single morning. I would go to bed at nine and wake up at two in the morning and drive twenty miles to the rest stop to pick up 500 newspapers that I would have to put together and deliver. Mind you, this was every single morning before high school. I have stories for days about that venture. The point is I was making about $3500 every month in high school because I was addicted to having the money to have the freedom.

Once I graduated from high school, I moved back down to San Diego City. I attended Grossmont Community College from 1996 to 1998. My plan was to get my associate's degree in general education, then transfer to San Diego State University to earn my bachelor's in criminal justice. The plan was to become an FBI agent. In between transferring from Grossmont to San Diego State University, I got a job as a personal trainer at a gym franchise. Remember those muscle magazines? I was broke as a joke and needed to make money to pay rent and eat, so I went with what I knew.

That job at the gym was a life-changer. I became the highest-selling trainer within my first few months. I was already making as much as I would have made if I were an FBI agent and having a blast while making own schedule. That's all I needed to experience before deciding to not return to college. My mom was disappointed at first, but she also knew how happy I was working at the gym. She was cool about it in the long run.

As a trainer, I met some of the coolest people who ended up changing my life. Three of these people were mentors who would change my career path immediately. One was a real estate financial loan officer, one was a CPA and real estate investor, and the third owned his own head-hunting company. All were very successful and made enough to pay my personal training fees, so I knew it was worth listening to them.

The lender would give me one hundred dollars for every person I sent to him who applied as was approved a home loan. I was down for it and started sending him two to four new clients per month. After a couple of months, he pulled me aside and said that he was very thankful for all the referrals. He mentioned that he gave all these buyers to real estate agents he knew because none of them had an agent. He told me I should get my license and help them. So that's what I did, I would go home every day and study for the real estate exam. After a little more than two months, I took the test and passed on my first try. It was game on from there! I was on my journey to financial freedom and a lifestyle that I could not have imagined as a child.

FREEDOM AND OPTIONS

This is what making money gives you—FREEDOM and OPTIONS. The more money you make, save, and invest, the more choices and freedom you have. The more choices you have, the more freedom

"Freedom is the Oxygen of the soul."

– MOSHE DAYAN

you have. When you're broke and have no money, you have to rely on others for survival. You are dependent on others. When you live in poverty, you are living from lack and constantly living out of fear. Fear that you may not make it another day, month, or year. The release of cortisol creates stress every day and negatively affects your life, the lives of those around you, and the quality of your day-to-day decisions. When you are in this poverty mindset, you can't create and thrive.

Humans have a few basic needs that need to be met. The specific number can be debated, but for the sake of this book and our goals, we will say there are three basic needs. Those are food, shelter, and sex/companionship. When you live from a perspective of lack, you constantly think of fulfilling only these three needs. However, when you have these needs covered, you can live from abundance, which releases happy chemicals in your body, including dopamine, endorphins, serotonin, and oxytocin. When you have the basic needs met, you can always live from a mindset of abundance, which I highly recommend.

The point is when you have money in the bank and have the ability to have these needs met daily, monthly, and yearly, you are in a different mindset, not one of scarcity but one of plenty. You can focus on the life you want. Do the things you really want and love to do. Spend time with the people you really want to and not people you have to. Your conversations will be different. You can tap back into your creative self, which is robbed from you the minute you become an adult with responsibilities.

Have you ever noticed that when you become a responsible adult, you start giving up the activities and interests you had as a child? Think back to when you were a child. What did you enjoy doing? Riding your bike? Playing the piano? Competing in sports? Drawing? Painting? Collecting something?

INTRODUCTION

But being a responsible adult means bills, not fun and games. And bills mean hours at a job. And a job means you earn a check to pay your bills. You are an adult now and responsible for the basic needs that your parents aren't taking care of for you anymore. The fun and games are over for now, and it's time to become independent and abandon what we used to love doing. But do we have to abandon them?

We all have something we used to do that we miss doing. The goal is to have the option to engage in those actives and interests again if we choose. Having these options makes us feel alive. We feel young and vibrant and much less stressed. We should all strive for this type of life. When we see people living like this, we tend to envy them and sometimes become jealous. The sad part is we feel we could never achieve what they have because we aren't as "lucky" or successful.

My goal in writing this book is not only to show you some known and proven strategies to make six figures in your real estate career, but it's also to show you how to become a person who can do anything you put your mind to by applying the same strategies to any part of your life. I have been selling real estate for almost seventeen years and studying personal development and growth for twenty years. Success, learning, and personal development all go hand-in-hand. To become the best, you must constantly improve yourself. Sharpen your mind every day in every way. Feed your mind and body the best ingredients every day and be conscious of them. What you put in is what you get out. If you put in bad information, you will get out bad information. If you eat processed foods that aren't good for you, you won't operate at your full potential.

The question is, can you learn to be in this positive state after childhood? The answer is an absolute YES. It is much harder as an adult and well worth it. Like anything else of significant worth,

"We cannot solve our problems with the same thinking we used when we created them."

— ALBERT EINSTEIN

INTRODUCTION

it takes a lot of work, time, and grit. When I say work, I mean working on everything in your life. Be intentional about improving your mindset, physical health, finance, skills, spirituality, and relationships. To become the best version of yourself, you must be the best version of yourself in every aspect as much as possible. Don't worry; we'll cover each of these in turn.

MINDSET

Mindset is the basis of success in all aspects of life. Without a clear, strong, positive, and committed mindset, accomplishing your real estate goals will be next to impossible. Even if you were to obtain success at some level, it will come and go without the correct mindset. That's why when people win the lottery, 70 percent go broke within three to five years. It's wasn't the money; it was the lack of the correct mindset to handle it. Your mind needs to be prepared and equipped for success. You need to sharpen your mental axe before you can chop down the biggest trees. Your mental axe is your mind, which includes your brain and attitude.

Are you optimistic or pessimistic? Do you look at the glass as half empty, half full, or both? We have the power to develop any mindset we want through training, practice, and consistency. Most of your mindset was developed by your parents and those around you, and your environment while you were an adolescent. It was by default. You had no choice.

You do have the choice to change. You do have the choice to step outside yourself, analyze and audit your mindset, and see what those around you see and perceive. You can start studying those you admire, paying close attention to the traits they possess and start inheriting these traits for yourself. Develop within you the kind of person you want to be. It all starts with the right mindset and a vision. The right mindset and the control of it. It's very simple, just not easy. It will take a lot of uncomfortable work and time. You will want to give up and quit. You will want to blame others. STOP! Accept responsibility and start working. It's the only way. Build the discipline muscle. You're the only person that can make the changes needed to become the person you want to become. You have the power to train that little voice in your head to listen to you and your commands. Your mind is powerful; treat it as such. Train it to listen and obey. It takes practice like anything else. Start NOW!

Physical Health

Without your physical health, what do you have? I see too many people get financially successful and let their health go. You only get one body, so you must take care of it as such. It's your temple. Please, please do not take it for granted. You need to be physically strong and running on all cylinders to perform at your best. It takes a lot of energy to become successful both physically and emotionally.

You need to be feeding your body the best foods possible to ensure it operates at the level you need. You must work out or do something physical every day. If you don't use your body physically, you'll lose it. Also, water is extremely important to your well-being. The goal is to drink eight ounces of water during every hour that you are awake, but in this case, more is even better. Carry around a reusable water bottle that you can fill up as needed. You can also fill a gallon jug and mark how much you intend to drink and by what time. Your body is made of up to 60 percent water. According to H. H. Mitchell, T. S. Hamilton, F.R. Steggerda, and H. W. Bean, in volume 158 of the *Journal of Biological Chemistry*, the brain and heart are composed of 73 percent of water, lungs are about 83 percent of water, the skin is 64 percent of water, muscles and kidneys are 79 percent, and the bones are 31 percent. As you can see, water is

"If you do not make time for your wellness, you will be forced to make time for your illness."

– UNKNOWN AUTHOR

very important to your temple; make sure you keep it fresh, clean, and consistent. If you can, try to drink as much distilled water as possible. It contains no contaminants. Starting, replace one soda or one juice with water. In my opinion, if you drink eight glasses of fluid a day, six should be water. Coffee is great as well because it's natural, has zero calories, and gives you energy.

You are what you eat! Have you heard this before? What are you eating? Many people eat and drink unnatural processed, chemical-filled, fried, candy, chips, soda, most fast food, pizza, and alcohol, and think it's ok; it isn't. Occasional cheats are acceptable but must be limited and based on your goals. However, 90 percent of your food should come from fruits, veggies, seeds, nuts, clean meats, if any, and eggs, coffee, and water. You can combine them however you want; just make sure you are getting clean, organic food from the Earth. The cleaner and more natural the food, the better you will feel and operate as a human. When grocery shopping, try to stay at the edges of the store. The aisles are typically filled with processed foods.

PRO TIP: *Only shop on the perimeter of the store. That's where all the fresh food is on display.*

The body works best when it's healthy and always working. Yes, you will get sore; that's why you must stretch and get into a sauna and become friends with cold water. Treat your body as if you only get one for your entire life because you do.

PRO TIP: *TAKE COLD SHOWERS! It will improve circulation and help you build discipline.*

"If you don't get serious about money, you'll never have serious money."

– GRANT CARDONE

PERSONAL FINANCE

How well do you do with finances? Do you live paycheck to paycheck? Are you maxed out on your credit cards? Do you drive a car you can barely afford and that you probably shouldn't have? It's time to do a reality check.

Money is the oxygen to your life and future. As much as some hate it and say it's the root of evil, we still need it just as bad as we need air to survive. This is the way life and society have been set up. If you have the connections to use a barter system or some other type of currency to get what you need to survive, more power to you. For the majority, money is the only tool we have to use as a collective society to trade. Money is a tool; use it as such.

Money is at the top of the list for all divorces, stress-related issues, inmates in prison, police forces, military forces, etcetera. The reason why is because people don't understand money. They don't actually use it for daily needs; they use it for wants. There's nothing wrong with wanting luxuries and having hobbies that cost money. The problem is when it interferes with your daily life or when it causes stress to you, your family, and those around you.

There's a funny thing that happens when you actually save enough money to cover your bills for twelve months. Your conversations are different, and your relationships are different. You start living instead of surviving. You start doing the things you love to do instead of what you are forced to do to survive. It frees up time and mental space for what we should be doing: living. If you believe money is bad, change your relationship with it now. Money is not evil. It's what people do with it that is.

One of the ways real estate agents get in trouble with their business is their taxes. You receive a 1099 for each transaction in real estate, which means you are responsible for paying your taxes. It's very common for an agent to get to the end of the year and realize

INTRODUCTION

they didn't save anything for taxes. The last thing you want is the IRS breathing down your neck when you're trying to build and run your business. I am not an accountant, a CPA, or in any position to give tax advice. I highly recommend speaking with your tax professional as soon as possible to create a tax plan. The sooner you do this, the easier life will be.

I will say that you need to keep your financial house in order. You will be a better real estate agent if you are not worried about rising gas prices when driving potential homeowners all over town. Save as much money as possible as soon as possible early in your career. Most agents want to go out and start buying new cars, new clothes, new gadgets, as soon as they start making money. As I've said before, set a goal to have a minimum of six to twelve months of your overhead in your bank account before spending money on things you don't absolutely need.

SKILLS/LEARNING

What makes one person's mind more valuable than the next person's, especially in the world of work and performance? SKILLS! Yes, the number of skills and the level to which you can use these skills make you valuable. Once you have the skills, are they in high demand? Can your skills solve big problems? These are questions you need to ask yourself. The better skills you have and the more problems they solve, the more you will get paid. Society rewards those who can solve the most prominent problems.

How do you gain skills or improve your current skill set? There are two basic ways: your experience or learning from someone else. You either have to experience more to get better, or you can learn from someone else's experience by reading books, listening to podcasts, watching YouTube videos, and by listening to those that are in a type of position you want. We all have access to most of the

"If you are not willing to learn, no one can help you. If you are determined to learn, no one can stop you."

— ZIG ZIGLAR

INTRODUCTION

above-mentioned for free or for an inexpensive fee to gain access. Take advantage! Learn as much as you can. Not just about your area of interest, but of everything. The more you know, the better you can connect with people and build rapport. The better you build rapport, the more people will want to be around you, and the more they will pay you. Become obsessed with becoming the best at what you do. Be known in your city for the skills you are paid for, and again, the way you do that is through learning and experience.

SPIRITUALITY

Spirituality means a lot of different things to a lot of different people. I don't necessarily mean religion when talking about spirituality, although it can be. I mean the understanding of life and what it means to you. What's your purpose in life? What makes you happy and grounded? Are you most at peace being with yourself or connecting with your environment and those around you?

Maintaining a healthy level of spirituality is understanding and controlling your ego and emotions as much as possible. Working on your self-awareness and empathy is an intention that you can work toward in a variety of ways. Some meditate. Some pray. Some read. Some go out in nature. Some go on vacation. Some surf. Some just sit with themselves. Some do whatever it is that brings them that deep sense of self. The key is to have your own outlet that allows you to connect and really get to know yourself. You don't have to be alone on top of a mountain to be spiritual, nor do you have to follow any particular group or mantra. You do have to block out time to work on it. Finding peace within yourself is very important, especially in the attention-stealing environment we live in today. I read recently that the average human today has an attention span of five seconds. When you look at it that way, increasing your focus

"Create a life that feels good on the inside, not one that just looks good on the outside."

— UNKNOWN

INTRODUCTION

through spirituality is a skill that will put you levels higher than other real estate agents.

RELATIONSHIPS

Last but not least, look at your relationships with people. When I say people, I mean everyone. Your friends, family, husband, wife, partner, kids, co-workers, the waitress who served you lunch, your clients, siblings, bosses, and everyone else with whom you've interacted. Please focus on having rich, caring relationships with as many people as possible. It's okay to have your differences and even not care to be around certain people. But, you still must learn to get along and look for the positive in those relationships as well. Learn to build strong relationships and work on your emotional intelligence. Become empathetic. Learn about people and how to connect while building rapport.

People want to be heard, and the problem is most just want to talk about themselves. We've all done it. You are having a conversation with someone, and you're just waiting for them to stop talking so you can say what you have to say. We're all guilty of this. Learn to be interested in people first, and then they will be interested in you. If you ask enough questions, you can always find something in common to connect with them. That's the goal, and to do it authentically.

Why do some people respond differently to what one person says or does versus another person? Instead of judging, learn to understand. Learn to put yourself in other people's shoes. Develop empathy. There are plenty of books to help with this. There are quotes and people you've probably heard before that push this concept. It's nothing new. Seek to understand and then to be understood.

> "What you do not want done to yourself, do not do to others."
>
> — CONFUCIUS

INTRODUCTION

How do you look in all of the areas we covered? How are you doing in your mindset, physical health, finance, skills, spirituality, and relationships?

Satisfactory? Need improvement? I'm sure there's a little of both, and my goal is to help you get 1 percent better every day. Each small improvement will eventually add up to tremendous results and a new life. A life in which you control and can move forward. A business by design that is worth having that you can run for as long as you want and need. A business that places you in the top 1 percent of all earners, especially in real estate. It will not be easy, but it will be worth it. Your family, friends, and coworkers will notice the changes. Be prepared to hear it because some will love it, and some will hate it. You will lose some people close to you. People do not like change. The closest people around you will hopefully be happy that you've chosen to take control, be successful, and own your life. Let's get started!

3 POWER QUESTIONS TO ASK YOURSELF

1. Why did you get into real estate?
2. On a scale of one to ten where "ten" is strongly committed, how committed are you to becoming a six-figure real estate agent?
3. Out of mindset, physical health, finance, skills, spirituality, and relationships, which areas do you need to improve most?

THE PATH OF A REAL ESTATE AGENT

I wanted to cover something I've noticed while watching new agents go from their first day as licensed real estate agents up until they are six-figure producers and beyond. My first agent has been with me since 2016. My newest recruit has been on the team for two months as I write this.

I've broken their journey loosely into seven stages. All my agents have experienced these same feelings at these stages. Many of my newer agents indicate they have already experienced the first and second stages prior to joining my team, and there are some who experience those two stages within two months of working with me. I focused on this observation because I wanted to create an expectation for the newer agents. I wanted them to know what feelings to expect when they started and progressed so when they felt it, they could address it and use it as a sign to keep pushing and a sign they were on the right track.

The Three Feet from Gold Rule—that's the rule. Most people give up and stop mining right before they are going to reach the jackpot. Same with everything else in life that's worth pursuing, the people who are disciplined and have the grit to keep going when everything feels like it's going to fail. These people keep pushing because they know what's on the other side of that pain.

Here are the seven stages of a new real estate agent:

Stage 1: Pre-Licensed or Freshly Licensed Real Estate Agent. Excited and ready to crush it! You heard about the real estate lifestyle and want answers. You'll show everyone what you are made of once you're licensed or now that you're licensed. At this stage, you typically expect real estate to be like going to medical school to become a doctor. You get your M.D. and apply to hospitals; the hospitals give you patients, and you start with a six-figure income. That's not how it works in this industry. Not at all. Getting your real estate license costs a few hundred dollars, and anyone can pass the test. There. I said it. You also realize that every brokerage is willing to offer you a job. You think you've made it, and the good life is ahead, but at this stage, that is extremely naïve thinking.

INTRODUCTION

Stage 2: First Week of Life as a Real Estate Agent. Still excited but confused and frustrated. There's no clear plan. There are a bunch of different strategies and tactics everyone says you should use to get clients. You don't know where to start and the brokerage you joined didn't give you any "clients" to work with like you thought. It's all on you. From the pens and paper to the business cards, to the computer, to the forms, the signs, the accountability, the paper on which you print, the office space, insurance, any and all of the apps you will need, the marketing—all of it is all on you. This first week is when you start to realize how it works, and it's not what you thought.

Stage 3: A Few Months into Life as a Real Estate Agent. Excitement has started to fade at this point and turns into deeper frustration. You feel like you're doing enough. You've told your friends and family about what you do. You've put up a few posts. You've held a few open houses, and still, NOTHING. The best thing you've got was an investor who told you he's buying up everything off-market under $300,000 in San Diego. The problem is he's told every other agent as well.

The situation is looking grim. You begin blaming everyone for why you're not succeeding. You assert that the agents that are getting business are "lucky," and you start looking around at other brokerages and thinking maybe it's the brokerage. Then you start thinking "Maybe this real estate profession isn't for me." This stage is where most people quit or fall into financial trouble due to no income. This can be the breaking point for most, but this is when you need to double down. Right before you feel like nothing is going your way, **KEEP GOING.**

PRO TIP: *There's an ancient Japanese technique called The Kaizen Way. This technique basically breaks down habits into the smallest parts possible. For example, if one wanted to start going to the*

> gym to get in shape, they wouldn't just start going every day at five o'clock in the morning and work out for two hours and eat broccoli and fish all day. Yes, that would definitely work; however, it is much too unreasonable for the untrained person. They would hurt themselves or get burned out. Research has proven that time and time again. Just look at New Year's resolutions. Forbes says that 80 percent of people that make New Year's resolutions fail year after year. The Kaizen Way allows you to break the resolution down into the smallest bites. What does that mean? It means get your membership and go to the gym and walk around the first day. Get a feel of the gym. Learn your way around. Day Two, come in and stretch for twenty minutes and go home. Light stretch. Day Three, stretch for ten minutes, walk slowly on the treadmill for two minutes, and go home. Day Four, stretch for ten minutes, four minutes on the treadmill, and go home. You will want to do more each time you go. It's in our nature to do more. To push ourselves. Use the Kaizen Way to start all the habits recommended in this book and anything other habits you want to form or lose.

Stage 4: First Client and Escrow. Then it happens. You kept pursuing relentlessly and picked up your first client off a video you did about buying your first home. (I just got goosebumps because this happens all the time.) You help him get approved; you work for a couple of weeks searching for the perfect home, and BOOM, you're in escrow. The excitement is back! You're on fire. You finally feel the rush of your first escrow. You're part of the "escrow" team. Ahhh. Feels nice, doesn't it? You're employed. (In real estate, you're technically unemployed if you have no homes in escrow because you have no paychecks coming your way.) Your excitement shows, people start to see your confidence, and you pick up two or three more clients over the next several months. It feels like people finally

INTRODUCTION

know who you are and what you do. You've made it! Or have you just begun?

Stage 5: Plateau. Your phone stops ringing. The referrals have stopped. You've closed those two or three pending deals and now crickets. No potential clients in the pipeline, and none seem to be coming in the near future. In real estate, you are typically thirty days from getting paid if you have no clients under contract to purchase or sell. The excitement starts to fade and turn into frustration again. This is another quitting point for most newer agents. They stopped following the schedule that got them to this point. The lead-generating activities have stopped, and they basically have to start all over again at Stage 3.

Stage 6: Two Years in. At this point in your career, you understand the game. You have the discipline and habits in place as a foundation to continue to crush your goals. You've made it this far because you know what needs to get done to generate leads and business. You struggle now to have another breakthrough to the next level of production. This is the new frustration. You will have highs and lows. These are the typical ebbs and flows of the real estate business. Your goal should be to minimize those ebbs and maximize the flows to keep a steady stream of business by sticking to the schedule. It's not easy, but it is simple.

Stage 7: Repeat the process. As you repeat the process, you learn to master your schedule, time blocking, and lead-generating activities. This allows you to carry more escrows at once. At this point, grow your business until you're at the desired income and production you wish. You may also decide to hire an assistant, a showing specialist, or start a team. However, starting a team is a whole different animal that we will talk about later.

It will be different for everyone, but this is what I have noticed with the agents I have coached and trained over the years.

When I show them these stages, they all agree. The faster you can get through them, the better. I tell you the stages so you can recognize when you are passing through each stage and so you are mindful, aware, prepared, and understand what's happening so you can keep moving forward.

3 POWER QUESTIONS

1. Which stage are you currently in?
2. What will be your plan when you reach the frustration point?
3. What is the next level of production you need to reach?

READY YOUR MIND

"The first hour of the morning is the rudder of the day."

– HENRY WARD BEECHER

CHAPTER 1

MORNING RITUAL

Set Up Your Day to WIN!

One of the common trends between all successful people that I've studied is their morning ritual. They are all adamant about their morning rituals and live by them. What does a successful morning ritual look like? What does your morning ritual look like? Do you just get out of bed at any time? Do you have a set plan or ritual that you follow every single morning that sets you up for success? These are all questions you need to ask yourself if you're looking to not only the best version of yourself but also a real estate professional that is making six figures a year. Now I'm not saying that you must have a morning ritual in place to be successful and make six figures; what I'm saying is it will highly improve your chances. I've studied hundreds of millionaires and successful people, read dozens of books, and attended hundreds of hours of lectures on what it takes to become at the top of the profession—not only for real estate, but with any competitive profession you can think of whether it be an attorney, a professional athlete, a business owner, a writer, producer, or any other career where there's competition.

The average person wakes up and lets the day run them instead of them running their day. They are constantly in reaction mode when they should be responding. "What's the difference?" you ask. When you are in reaction mode, you react to everything and everyone around you based on their schedules. This creates stress and anxiety while releasing the stress chemical cortisol. When you work from a response mode, you're getting back to them on your schedule and with your chosen level of importance.

We either have morning rituals that are beneficial and add value or morning rituals that keep us unorganized, stressed out, and stagnant. The clearer your mind, the clearer your thinking. Remember the two easiest and quickest times your brain is primed for learning that are mentioned in the introduction? That's right: morning and evening! The clearer you're thinking, the more focused and successful you will be. Imagine with me for a second two different scenarios and two different morning rituals. Put yourself in both scenarios, and the most crucial part is to be 100 percent honest with yourself. It's the only way this will work.

SCENARIO #1

You go to bed at midnight and get up at eight in the morning. You lie in bed, check your email, respond to a couple of urgent messages, mindlessly check your social media for twenty minutes, realize you're late, and jump in the shower. Next, you throw some clothes on and eat a shitty breakfast that consists of anything you can get your hands on, which most of the time is a bad choice. Then you wash it down with a cup of coffee or an energy drink to make sure you have the vigor to get you through the next eight hours of work. Before you know it, the day is over, and you're overwhelmed with the number of tasks that you didn't complete for the day. You add these tasks to the next day. This continues to happen repeatedly until it's out of control and you become stressed out.

What happens when you're stressed out? You take it out on your friends, family, and coworkers, and you're overall a miserable person that no one wants to be around. Is this you? Do you know someone like this? It's not fun for you or anyone around you. These people typically don't even like themselves. I'm not saying there aren't people out there who aren't happy or successful who sleep those hours. I'm just speaking of probabilities. There's a better way that's been tried and proven over time with tons of people to back it.

SCENARIO #2

You wake up at four o'clock with a ton of energy; it's still dark outside. You roll over and put on a motivational speech on YouTube. As you're lying in bed, listening to the positive discourse coming through your smart phone, you think of everything you're grateful for in your life at that moment and for all the experiences that make you the person you are today. Nothing bad or good has ever happened to you. We only make it good or bad by the label or idea we have of it. For example, if someone gave you one hundred dollars in San Diego, it really wouldn't change your life. That same one hundred dollars given to a kid barely surviving in a third-world country could literally change their life. Being grateful and listening to motivational speeches sets your day up for a positive mindset that will set the pace and standard for the rest of your day.

Next, you jump out of bed, get dressed in your gym clothes that are already sitting next to the bed. You make your way to the kitchen where your day is set up and ready for you to take action. You fill up a glass of water and set it next to your book, your goal writing journal, and your creative activity. As you drink your water, you're writing your goals and affirmations down. When you're done writing your goals and affirmations, you begin reading a book, and for every two pages you read, you do fifty push-ups in between flipping the pages. When you are done with at least thirty pages of reading (increase this number over time), you put your headphones on and listen to some more affirmations while you go for a run. After your run, you return home, take your vitamins and drink another glass of water. Jump in the shower and get to work.

Which day sounds like a top performer's day? It should be easy to figure out this one. Imagine if the second scenario was your day—every day. Be honest with yourself. Do you think you would be more successful? More productive? A better version of yourself? Could you feel healthy and have more energy? I think it's safe to say "Yes!" Let's break down each part of your morning.

> **PRO TIP:** *Set up your environment to WIN. Choose a quiet area in your home and carefully set it up to win the day. Do it at the same time every morning in the same place. Have a full glass of water, notebook for goals, current reading material, YouTube, gym clothes set out next to your bed the night before, coffee or a pre-workout supplement ready to drink, vitamins, and anything else you incorporate into your winning schedule. Having everything set-up to win leaves no excuses. It's being proactive and having intention. It's having control over your success.*

WAKE UP

I used to be like most people: I dreaded getting up in the morning, loved my sleep, and wished I could sleep forever. Sleep is the best feeling until it isn't. When you don't have anything that excites you, that you can't stop thinking about, sleep is the next best thing

"Wake up early every day so that while others are dreaming, you can make your dreams come true."

– HAL ELROD

to sex, especially if you are lucky enough to have someone to wake up next to whom you love. Do me a favor; imagine with me for a minute back to when you were a child. Imagine when your parents told you that the next day you were going to Disneyland or it was your birthday or your first day of middle school. How did you feel? If you were anything like me, you couldn't sleep, and you woke up every hour staring at the clock, hoping time would pass faster so you could get up and get going.

If it was your first day of school, you had your new favorite clothes out, ready to show off to all your friends. Or you were thinking of what rides you would go on first at Disneyland and how it would make you feel ... the good old days when life was so simple. So easy. Now imagine if you had that feeling as an adult. It is Sunday night, and you cannot wait to get up on Monday morning and go to work. The great news is it can be. That's why morning rituals are so important. They set-up your day and create the energy and vibe for the day. It can be positive, inspiring, and motivating, or it can be pessimistic, negative, and unproductive. It's a choice only you get to make. Make it a positive one.

WHAT TIME DO YOU WAKE UP?

I used to wake up between seven thirty and eight o'clock every morning Monday through Friday and sleep until nine o'clock or ten o'clock on the weekend mornings. Sometimes later, if I went out drinking the night before and was feeling like shit and hungover. I thought this was normal. I would tell myself that I was living the life. I got to sleep in, wake up when I wanted, and on my terms. I would say to myself the same thing I hear everyone else say, "I'm not a morning person." Is this you or someone you know? I guarantee you know someone that says this. It's bullshit. Someone made that up to justify waking up late. They told themselves that story

"Every morning you have two choices: Continue to sleep with your dreams, or wake up and chase them."

– CARMELO ANTHONY

enough times that they believed it. They heard their friends say the same thing. It made sense, so you just went on and believed it. When someone gives me this excuse, I ask, "What if I told you I would give you $50,000 if you were at my house tomorrow morning at four o'clock?" Every single person has an aha moment. They realize that they just don't have the right motivation. They haven't found their *why*. They haven't found a powerful enough reason to get up. It's a paradigm shift. Would you be at my house at four o'clock in the morning for $50,000? Three o'clock in the morning? Yes, you would.

And what would happen after you woke up at half past seven or eight o'clock in the morning? You would lay in bed for a while, check your phone, and slowly get up while rushing at the same time to get to work. Rushing to get in the shower, rushing to get dressed and out the door without eating, or eating shitty food that had no real nutritional value and gave you no sustainable energy. Let's not forget you're in reaction mode. You are reacting to your phone, emails, text messages, kids, partner, clients, etcetera. Now your whole day feels rushed and frustrating while you're downing coffee and energy drinks to stay awake. This affects the way you are interacting with your friends, family, and co-workers. Does this sound familiar? I remember it all too clearly. Are my days always perfect? No. Somedays, I'm rushing around downing energy drinks. Not preferred, but when I don't follow my regular routine, this seems to be my default. I am constantly improving, and I'm okay with that. As long as you are progressing forward, you are on track.

Why would anyone want to get up that early each morning including weekends, holidays, and birthdays? Does this sound like torture? It probably does to most people that normally get up after seven o'clock in the morning. It's a dramatic change. Why would anyone in their right mind choose, yes, *choose* to do this? This was my exact thought when I first heard it.

I've been studying the super successful billionaires, game-changers, champions, innovators, elite athletes, business owners, and everyone who lives the life most call "lucky" for a while, and one thing they all had in common was their morning rituals. YES! Their morning rituals. They all would get up at uncomfortable times in the mornings. The average billionaire was getting up at four o'clock in the morning. I would read this and hear it, and again make excuses. They are nerds. They are boring and don't have a life. This was the story I was telling myself for years. Again, complete bullshit. All in my head. The natural instinct to be comfortable is in all of us. That's why so few many reach their true potential. If it's not broken, don't fix it. Improve it!

> **PRO TIP:** *Mel Robbins, author of* **The 5 Second Rule**, *states that if you have an instinct to act on a goal, you must physically move within 5 seconds, or your brain will kill it. She says the second you have the thought or urge to do something, count 5-4-3-2-1- GO and move towards your action immediately.*

What I realized was my vision and my goals were not aligned, something had to change, and waking up early was the first step. Why? What is the difference between waking up at half past three or half past seven in the morning? Both these times were still considered early for me, but I noticed one thing right away. **Distraction.** When I get up before four o'clock, there are absolutely no distractions. It's perfectly silent. My phone isn't ringing, text messages are not going off, emails aren't pinging, no children are playing, and nothing is pressing for me to get done right when I wake up. It's all me time—my alone time.

> "*Every morning starts a new page in your story. Make it a great one today.*"
>
> – DOE ZANTAMATA

I get to do the things I've never had time for, and I don't feel rushed. I get to take my time and do what I need and want to do. What is that? As I said before, the first thing you hear and think in the morning sets the tone of the day. The last thing you want to do when you wake up and check your emails is get a bad email. A canceled deal. Yelled at by a client. Missed a deadline, etcetera. So do not check emails yet. This is where building that discipline muscle comes into place. Like at the gym, the more you work this muscle, the stronger it gets. Start small, and work your way up.

MOTIVATION

Grab your phone first thing in the morning and put on some motivational videos to jumpstart your attitude and energy. I typically go to YouTube and type in motivation, motivational speech, business motivation, billionaire motivation, morning motivation, or anything similar. Some talks will resonate deeper than others. There are thousands of great videos you can find, and they're free. I recommend saving the ones you find that really get you going. You may find a particular person who gets you hyped; subscribe.

Here are a few to check out: Tom Bilyeu, Ed Mylett, Grant Cardone, Jordan Peterson, Tony Robbins, Eric Thomas, Les Brown, Brian Tracy, Simon Sinek, Jim Rohn, Zig Ziglar, David Goggins, Jordan Belfort, Bob Proctor, Earl Nightingale, and Napoleon Hill are just a few I listen to and recommend. Build a collection of these go-to videos and save them. You will learn to love them, and they will set a positive, successful tone for your day. I've been doing it for years now, and it's game-changing. If you don't like YouTube, you can find motivational speeches and podcasts on iTunes or your favorite place to find music. **DO IT NOW.**

GET DRESSED TO GET PHYSICAL

The night before you go to bed set out your workout clothes for the following day. They should be on top of your workout shoes that are placed right at the side of your bed so when you sit up, they are directly in front of you. Do not get up until you have these clothes on, your shoes on, and your motivational speech playing. You are setting up your environment to win. The mindset to succeed for the day. These habits need to be in place to optimize your chances for the results you want and the goals you are after. Now that you're dressed, go brush your teeth and get away from your bed. Go to the area of the house you have set up for your morning ritual. I have my set up in my kitchen on the island. I fill up a glass of filtered water and set it next to the book I am reading and my journal and pen. I typically light a candle for ambiance. I start by taking a huge gulp of water to get my system going and help wake me up. Water is the first thing that should be put into your body every morning to help get your metabolism going and wake you up.

GET DRESSED FOR SUCCESS

You're done with the gym and finished eating and showering; now it's time to dress for success. What does that mean? It means I wore three-piece suits for the first thirteen years of my career. Do you need to wear a three-piece suit? Depends on your goals and your market. Who is in your client community? Dress for them, and then consider things like the weather and the occasion. Who are you meeting today? This can be tricky. I've had some clients that didn't want me in a suit at all. They would get weird when I showed up in a suit. I've also had clients who felt offended because I wasn't dressed to the 9's with a suit and tie. Another thing to consider is your market. If you are working the beach, a suit may be overkill.

"Dress the way you want to be addressed."

— JEFF DISCHER

"People who wrote down their goals were 42% more likely to achieve them than the ones who didn't. Telling a friend increases this rate to 78%."

— DR. GAIL MATTHEWS

If you're working in the city, a Tommy Bahama shirt may not be a sufficient portrayal of your professionalism.

I tell my agents there are two first impressions: the way you look and what you say. What does that mean? It means that if you are a newer agent and perhaps insecure about what you're saying because you're inexperienced and lack the knowledge, then looking the part is much more important at that moment. You need to overcompensate for your lack of knowledge base. On the other hand, if you've been selling for a while and have the experience, what you say can overpower how you look. I can assume if you are reading this book, you are a newer agent—**DRESS WELL!**

> **PRO TIP:** *If ever in doubt about what to wear, overdress for the occasion.*

WRITE DOWN YOUR GOALS

Do you write your goals? I write my goals every single day. I write them and say them out loud as I'm writing them. There is science behind the difference between having goals, writing goals, and writing down and saying your goals aloud. Just writing our goals down increases you achieving them by 42 percent. A Harvard Business School study found that 3 percent of graduates that wrote down their goals ended up earning ten times as much as the other 97 percent put together just ten years after graduation. I could write an entire book on goals. I have been writing my goals for years, and the clearer I am, the better.

One of the habits I created for myself is to write my goals and affirmations as one. For example, I will write "I am a writer. I will write two pages per day and will write a #1 best-selling book by December 31, 2021." You get the idea. It may be tough at first, but it will get easier as you go. I encourage my team and those I train and coach to use the S.M.A.R.T. (specific, measurable, achievable, relevant, and timely) goal writing system. (For more on S.M.A.R.T. goals, see Appendix B: Write Down Your Goals.)

Another key is not to look at yesterday's goals. Goals will change. The most important goals will come to mind every day. If there are goals from yesterday that aren't on your list today, they weren't relevant today. What you wrote down today is relevant and what's important. That's ok, go with it. Adjust and accept the new goals and get to work.

READ

After I'm done writing my goals and affirmations, I begin to read a non-fiction book. I'm looking to fuel and build my brain. To expand it. Books based on business and personal development are the type of books I prefer. The more you learn, the more you earn. Reading has changed my life, and it will change yours. Every super successful person I have studied has been a lifetime learner and avid reader. It's a common thread between all of them. I'm not saying you MUST read to become successful; I'm saying it increases your chances by a lot. Set a goal for yourself to read a certain number of pages a day. If you don't read or haven't read for a while, start small with around five pages per day. It will be tough. It will demand patience and focus. Like a muscle, the ability to focus becomes better over time. You build on it. Before you know it, you're reading thirty to fifty pages per day, every day. It's very addictive because you see the benefits and the difference in your conversations and understanding. It becomes something you look forward to doing every day. You find yourself buying more books than you can read. I have stacks of books around my house and office that I still need to read. Another way to get in additional reading is through listening

"Reading is the gateway skill that makes all other learning possible."

– BARACK OBAMA

to audiobooks. There are apps like Audible, 12 Minutes, Kindle, Apple Books, Blinkest, or whichever you prefer to help you get in additional knowledge while you're driving, exercising, traveling, or any other activity that allows you to listen.

My goal is to read twenty books per month. Yes, it's a lot. I didn't just wake up one day and start reading twenty books a month. I slowly built up to it. I do it like this: I read fifty to one hundred pages per day, which is a 200- to 250-page book every two or three days. I also listen to Audible on 2.5 speed, allowing me to listen to an eight-hour book in about three and a half to four hours. I can listen to about a book every two to three days. Between the two methods, I read ten to twelve paperbacks and listen to three to four Audible books per month. This will, by itself, change your life. Start with two books per month and build on it. It's like going to the gym; if you go and workout for two hours a day to start, you will burn out and get frustrated. Apply the Kaizen way, very small steps that slowly turn into large results. I would also encourage you to start with books that are easier to read. Self-help books are typically easier to read than most compared to a dense book on psychology that gets deep into complex concepts that demand complete focus and comprehension. Focus on books that are easy to digest. In-between my reading, I do fifty push-ups every time I turn a page. This is habit stacking. I'll get into that in a later chapter on habits. Basically, you can get multiple things done at once without taking away from each task, and it creates triggers. (For a list of the twenty-one books I recommend for business and life, see Appendix C: Readers are Leaders.)

> **PRO TIP:** *It's always easier to read something you're genuinely interested in, so when you first start reading consistently, start with books on subjects that interest you. Read about something you*

> *really want to know. I didn't like reading at all in school because I didn't like anything they were teaching. When I was twenty-one, I was given the book* What to Say When You Talk to Yourself *by Dr. Shad Helmstetter, that book alone turned me into a reader. As you become better at reading, you can step up to more advanced and denser books of various subjects.*

EXERCISE

Health is wealth! The healthier you are, the better you can perform. The better you can perform, the more you can get done. Don't fight me on this. There is also a level of respect that comes to those that take great care of themselves. A level of undeniable discipline. I believe that subconsciously people respect those who are physically fit because they know the amount of self-discipline, time, and work it takes to get there. What do you think when you see someone who looks great in clothes and can tell they are physically fit? If you hate, it's because you envy; if you respect, it's because you appreciate and know that's how you should look and feel. The way you look is a byproduct of how you feel. The way you feel, the amount of energy you have, the level of confidence you have, the better the posture, and the list goes on. So, what am I saying? I'm saying to get up and get physical! It's worth it, and you will thank me.

Getting physical doesn't have to be going for a ten-mile run, going to the gym for two hours, doing a boot camp yoga class, or any other super-intense activity; it means doing more than you're used to and building resilience and endurance. Start with a walk around the block, five push-ups and five sit-ups, and stretching for twenty minutes. Just get up and get active. I tell people to start small because it is tough. You will want to give up. Starting small allows

> "Anyone who stops learning is old, whether twenty or eighty. Anyone who keeps learning stays young."
>
> — HENRY FORD

"Exercise gives you endorphins."

– LEGALLY BLONDE

you to build up and make progress. As you make progress and begin to see results, you want to improve, and naturally, you will get better and more fit. Stick with it. You will start pushing yourself to accomplish more physically. You will be less sore, and you will feel the benefits. Please remember, this is a lifestyle change, not an end result. The end result comes when you are dead or incapacitated. Exercise must become a part of who you are like brushing your teeth. You brush your teeth so you don't lose them. Nobody likes a toothache. If you can take care of your teeth every day and shower every day, you can exercise.

Another action step is to track your progress and calendar your workouts. You should also write and track your starting points so you have a reference. Put it in your calendar as if your livelihood depended on it because it does. I also believe physical exercise should be done every single day. The reason I say every day is because it leaves no room for error. No days that you can slip and come back to it. Imagine not brushing your teeth every day! Exactly! Gross, right? Another way to make it easier is to find a workout partner to keep you accountable. If you don't have someone or can't find someone, use public accountability. Post it on social media for everyone to see. Let social media keep you accountable. This really works. People may make fun of you for posting every time you check into the gym, let them. That's their problem, not yours. You have a mission and lifestyle to maintain. Now go get it!

GET CREATIVE

Have you heard of the right brain versus the left brain? There is some debate on this concept; I believe it to be true to an extent. Researchers have documented that some people are more left-brained and logical, and some people are more right-brained and creative. I think there is some truth to this, but I also think you can

"Creativity is intelligence having fun."

– ALBERT EINSTEIN

train and build each side. As children, we tend to operate primarily from our creativity, in my opinion, due to not having any real-life responsibilities such as having to cover the costs of rent, food, car payment, and other bills. Have you ever noticed that as kids, you did more creative activities in general? Draw, paint, dance, sing, build, discover, explore, play musical instruments, etcetera. Then we become responsible adults, take on our own monthly responsibilities, and everything changes. We stop doing the things that were exciting and start using the left, logical side of the brain. We start worrying about covering our basic needs: food, shelter, companionship. It's not a bad thing; it does, however, rob you of activities you used to love. I believe those are where we find our passions. I challenge you to bring back something you used to love as a child. Start drawing again. Start painting. Start singing. Start playing an instrument. Anything that makes you feel like a kid again. Personally, I started taking piano lessons at the age of thirty-nine years old. I have lessons once a week, every week. Yes, there are days when it's tough, and I'm overwhelmed with my "responsibilities" as an adult, however, I still show up.

Again, your morning rituals and habits set the tone for your day and your future. Nothing I am recommending is new or guarantees results, but it does increase your probabilities for success and puts you in a much better position to achieve what you desire in life. What I've recommended are all options and suggestions that I perform and have received excellent results. These activities and suggestions have been collected, added to, and some subtracted to come up with my list. These action steps have been used by several highly successful people and recommended in over a hundred books that I have read. I challenge you to incorporate as many of these action steps and habits as possible into your life and into your morning ritual. Start slow if you are new to this type of morning schedule, and slowly add as you go. If you encounter any additional

MORNING RITUAL

activities that add to your overall success, health, and mindset, feel free to add away. Now get started!

> **3 ACTION STEPS**
>
> 1. Choose a time to wake up every morning, preferably before five o'clock, and stick to it. Consistency is key.
> 2. Set up your environment to win and remove anything that can derail your success.
> 3. Stack habits together. For example, put a glass of water next to your notepad for your goals, have a motivational video playing on YouTube, and put the book you're reading next to the notepad.

"Discipline is the bridge between goals and accomplishment."

– JIM ROHN

CHAPTER 2

DISCIPLINE AND HABITS

Show Me Your Habits, and I'll Show You Your Future

YOU'RE RESPONSIBLE

Now that we've talked about your morning rituals, let's dive deeper into the why you should incorporate these habits and disciplines and what exactly they do for you. As an agent, you are responsible for your schedule. You don't clock in and out. There's no salary or hourly pay as a real estate agent. You must make changes and be aware of the choices you are making on a daily basis. If you're not getting the results you want, something must change. It's easy for me to tell you to completely turn your comfortable mornings upside down and ask you to make huge changes, but why? Why does it matter what time you get up in the morning and what time you go to bed? How are your habits and disciplines tied directly to your success? Is there a reason you can't stay up every night until one o'clock in the morning and wake up seven hours later at eight o'clock and still be highly successful in all areas of life? These are all great questions. Do you believe your daily choices have any effect on your overall life? Your health? Your business? Your relationships? Your finances? Your future? Yes, this is a lot of questions; however, I must get your brain thinking and scrutinizing your current lifestyle, so you have some context for this chapter. One of my favorite quotes is, "Show me your habits, and I'll show you your future" by yours truly.

It's fairly self-explanatory. If you eat a breakfast burrito with a sugar-filled coffee for breakfast, a burger with fries and a soda for lunch, a candy bar in between lunch and dinner as a snack, and a large bowl of spaghetti for dinner every night, eventually you will be overweight and extremely unhealthy with some major health issues. In my opinion, these are bad habits, and anyone following this type of regime will eventually suffer. You can't deny history and facts. You probably know someone that has this lifestyle and has had complications with their health, and if they haven't, they will. It's inevitable. You may also know someone that has the opposite diet. Fresh fruit, coffee, and water in the morning; some nuts and seeds for snacks; a salad for lunch; and a piece of salmon and veggies for dinner while drinking water all day. These people typically have tons of energy, great skin, and look younger than their age. Diet also runs parallel with their workouts. People who eat like they don't care often don't take care of their physical bodies either. It's actually very sad because most of them don't feel the pain until it's too late. The type of person who has no awareness of their habits typically has no awareness of their future and how it affects their day-to-day lives. Your success starts with your health, which we'll cover in detail in a later chapter. Most people do one thing in life the way they do everything in life. If their cars are messy, their homes are messy, their desks are messy, and everything else about them is messy. That's why it's very important to start with something simple—like changing your small habits and building from there.

WE ALL HAVE HABITS

We all have habits. We either choose our habits, or they choose us. By default, we tend to choose habits that are easy and comfortable—habits that are immediately satisfying. A rule I've learned about habits is those that offer immediate gratification tend to provide long-term negative results, and those that provide long-term benefits tend to be immediately boring.

For example, if you earn one hundred dollars today, you can buy a new pair of shoes or go out for a nice meal. That feels good today. Thinking long-term means you take into consideration that you may need that money for more important matters in the future but will not have any money at the time you need it if you immediately spend it. On the other hand, if you make the same one hundred dollars and invest it today, while you may not immediately get the shoes or enjoy a fancy meal, you will have more opportunity in the future to enjoy such luxuries, and if correctly invested, that money will grow. If you eat a burger and fries every day for a few years, you will feel great while eating it, and it may be satisfying; but the long-term effects will be obesity, high blood pressure, bad skin, possibly heart issues, breathing issues, sleep issues, and more, resulting in hospital visits and expensive medical bills. The person who eats the clean diet might not be as satisfied while eating, and the meal may not be as fun; but overall, that person will feel better, look better, look younger, and have far fewer health issues. Learning to be

"A habit is a lifestyle to be lived, not a finish line to crossed."

– JAMES CLEAR

DISCIPLINE AND HABITS

aware and choose the best habits based on the life you want to live and being the best version of yourself are crucial.

Discipline and habits go hand-in-hand. If you are not disciplined, then you probably don't have great habits. One must be disciplined to create great habits. Discipline is the ability to train yourself to obey your choices and the control over your mind to know that what you are doing is the best choice based on your goals. If you're not disciplined, when it comes time to choose between the burger and the salad, you will just go with what is comfortable. Discipline allows you to have control over your choices without deviation.

It is not easy. As I said earlier, our mind and body want to do what's easy and comfortable by default. It's human nature. Discipline is also different than willpower. Willpower is more about the moment; discipline is more structured and part of a larger goal. Willpower wanes as the day passes; discipline is always on. You can work at developing and mastering discipline. Like anything, the more you practice and work at it, the better you get at it. It's an amazing concept. With a disciplined mindset, creating and building the right habits becomes a lot easier. You can literally step back and look at your life and see where the holes are and make the changes needed to create the life you want to achieve. You can say "yes" to what you want and "no" to that which is detrimental to your success.

Let's relate discipline to real estate and how it will help you get to six figures in twelve months. Most people who get into real estate think it's easy money and a lifestyle of glamour. This is true only if you have the proper life structure. A truly disciplined schedule with proven activities and habits can and will create a life worth living. It starts with your morning rituals, as explained in Chapter 1: Morning Ritual—Set Up Your Day to WIN, then runs into the rest of your day. We start with the morning because it sets your day up. It's basically stretching before you take off on a morning run.

The morning is about personal growth and setting up your mindset for the day to win. How do you set up your day? You write down how your perfect day looks. You take the activities you must do and make them a priority. See how close your life is to being that way and start making the changes to become the best version of that person. This will more than likely require changes to your schedule. To be the best, you must have the best habits.

NO FORMAL SCHEDULE

One way that real estate is different than most other professions or careers is that there is no formal schedule. For the most part, you can get hired by a real estate company and never show up, and more than likely, no one will ever check in with you. There is little to no accountability. It's one of the toughest ideas to accept and understand. I see it all the time, and it is probably one of the top reasons most people fail. They quit their 9-to-5 job, get licensed, get hired, and then basically think that deals will just fall into their lap.

New agents will start their new careers, and on day one, they will schedule a non-work-related appointment to do something like get their brakes repaired on their vehicle. When they were in their last job, though, they would have had to wait until the weekend, go on their lunch break, or go after work to take care of this kind of personal business. Suddenly, relishing in this newfound freedom and flexibility that their real estate calendars seemingly afford them, they believe they can simply go in the middle of a Monday on their first day on the job as an agent. And this blows my mind.

I know it sounds crazy, but this happens to seven out of ten new agents where they believe their time is truly their time to do whatever they want with. The key is to treat your real estate career like you had a boss because you do have one—YOU. Think about it as though you must be at the office with a list of duties to get

"The key is not to prioritize your schedule, but to schedule your priorities."

– STEPHEN R. COVEY

done or you will get fired. The truth is you are your own boss. You will have to fire yourself if you don't do the things necessary to get homes sold. You need to work a minimum of nine in the morning to five in the afternoon Monday through Sunday and then be accessible on your phone the rest of the time. You need to plug into your schedule the activities that need to get done and stick to them over a long period of time. Consistency is key and a major factor in your success.

Anyone who gets paid a six-figure income has put in a lot of work in some way or another. Doctors have eight to ten years of education and interning; attorneys have seven to eight years of school; veterinarians, dentists, airline pilots, business owners, high-level members of management, CEOs, etcetera all have had to put in the work. Some put it in with formal education, and some put it in with experience and slowly move up the ladder. Of course, there are some who fail their way to the top. The point is that real estate is no different. There are only three quick classes to get your real estate license, and BOOM, you're off to start your career. SO, where and how do you get the time? Where is all the education? Real estate is one of the easiest professions to get licensed in and make the most money in the least amount of time. It can be done. I've done it for myself and have helped numerous other agents do it as well. Earning six figures in real estate can either take you twelve months, twelve years, or never happen at all. It is up to you!

I know you want it in twelve months or sooner. I get it. This is where disciplined habits have their place. So how do you build your discipline muscle so you can rework your current habits? The same way you build your biceps or legs at the gym, you work. Let's start by identifying what your current habits are and where your level of discipline is. To do this, you'll need to scrutinize your day and pay attention to every single thing you do. Actually, you need to do this for a few days. When I say pay attention to every single thing,

DISCIPLINE AND HABITS

I mean everything. If you've never done this before, get ready. You are about to find out some things about yourself you didn't even know.

People often live their lives on auto-pilot, so when they start paying attention to their days, the good and bad habits stand out quite quickly. We start seeing where we waste time, where we waste money, why we are overweight and unhealthy, how good or bad our relationships are. The list goes on.

Let's start with the first thing in the morning. What time do you wake up, and why? What are the first things you do in the morning upon awakening? You can either write your notes on your phone or write them in a journal. You **MUST** be authentic and honest with yourself. Otherwise, as they say, you're only cheating yourself. So, write down everything you do from the minute you wake up until the minute you lay your head down to sleep, including what you eat. The gum you chewed. The beer you drank. Don't forget the time you spent mindlessly on social media getting absolutely nothing done. Do this for a few days to get a sense of your days and your habits. Pay attention to everything, and once you have it all written down, notice how hard it was to do the easy things. Was there ever a time when you knew you were making a bad decision and still made it? That's your discipline muscle not working.

Your current discipline plus your current habits are very powerful and will be hard to break without a structured plan in place. Once you incorporate a structured plan, you will either justify the good and the bad things you do, or you will find yourself in a state of shock, hoping the plan will eventually aid in making some of the changes easier. Please remember, this will not be easy. You are trained or have been trained to live a certain way without even knowing it. The good news is that you can change. You MUST want it bad enough, and with enough discipline and correct habits, you'll make that change. History has proven itself. Many of the most

"With self-discipline, most anything is possible."

– THEODORE ROOSEVELT

successful people in the world and in history have credited their highest levels of success to habits and discipline.

WE ARE NOT BORN WITH DISCIPLINE

We are not born with discipline. We learn it at a young age through our parents and those closest to us. We either learn good disciplines or bad disciplines. We have little control over who we learn from and when we learn it as a child. What happens when you get older and want to improve your self-discipline? You develop it. How do you develop discipline? You start small. You use the Japanese technique I mentioned earlier, The Kaizen Way. One percent better every day adds up quickly, especially when it's compounding, which is what it will do. Instead of getting up at seven in the morning, you get up fifteen minutes earlier at a quarter to seven. The following week, you get up at half past six in the morning. Then the next week, at six in the morning and so on until you are at the desired time. You start by reading one page a day. The next day, two pages; the next day, three pages; and so on. Again, we are building the discipline muscles of these activities. You are using discipline to develop the necessary habits for ultimate success. Once you complete the exercise of tracking your day and all activities, you will set new goals and document the changes you want and need to make. More than likely, you will require a change in most areas. You will be setting your large goals and ultimate changes, and then setting small intermediate milestones until you reach your final destination. Then you'll start over with bigger and better.

Have you ever been forced to use discipline? Our parents funnel it into us as children, and our school system backs them. You were disciplined to a certain degree as a child. You got up every morning for school, ate breakfast, took a shower, put on your clothes, and had to be in your classroom by a specific time—usually before the bell rang. Then throughout the day, you had to go to your next class, finish your next project, make it to the bus stop or out front of the school for your parents to pick you up, get home and do your homework, eat your dinner, brush your teeth, and go to bed, all so you could wake up the next day and do it again. You were disciplined and had a habit schedule. Both created a proper foundation required for an adolescent preparing to live in society. This forced discipline and accountability were necessary to get through life. Our parents, teachers, and anyone else responsible for our well-being and growth forced us by instilling consequences for not doing the required activities needed to get us to adulthood. Imagine a child with no schedule or discipline? The probability of that child becoming a contributor to society is much lower than those who were disciplined.

So why do our parents and teachers hold us accountable and instill a disciplined life? Is it because they want to see us fail? Is it because they don't care? Quite the opposite, they want us to succeed. Not only in school but in life. This discipline is not a control thing. It's a life thing. I know that if I had a child, I would be pushing the same thing. It's because discipline is what allows us to control what we do either bad or good. Discipline is the decision-making muscle that we must work on every day for the rest of our lives. It does get stronger over time, just like going to the gym and working out your biceps so they will grow and become stronger. This is what we must do for our discipline muscle.

Typically, those with the biggest muscles are the strongest. I truly believe that those with the most discipline have the most control in life. Those with discipline have the most freedom. How? Because they control their time and disciplined with their habits and schedule, there is no confusion. They use discipline to set goals, create the right habits, and work a schedule that enforces the ideal life. They schedule the most rewarding and powerful activities and

DISCIPLINE AND HABITS

get them done accordingly. They prioritize their habits and schedule to do the most important tasks first. Lack of discipline would have you doing what's easy and easy doesn't get the results we're looking for in this book. Lack of discipline will have you out drinking with your friends late the night before an interview or big project is due. Lack of discipline will allow you to get comfortable in life and business, and start slipping.

On the other hand, discipline will allow you to be crystal clear as to your objectives and cut through the activities and people that will bring no value. Discipline will have you doing lead generation, open houses, videos, showings, and every other real estate activity you should be doing to get the results you want. Discipline will also keep you in the best physical shape and eating only the best foods by sticking to a gym routine and eating schedule.

Discipline separates the six-figure agents from the barely-making-it agents. I know and have personally spoken with multiple high-producing agents in real estate, and a very common trend is the discipline and habits they have. This concept of discipline isn't just for real estate agents; these same thoughts about discipline and habits are also coming from my friends in other professional industries. These are attorneys, physicians, business owners, professional athletes, and many other elite performers. Discipline and habits literally separate the best from the average. I'm not saying the average doesn't have discipline; it may just be in the wrong areas of life. That's ok; these concepts are not for everyone. Not everyone was made or wants to be great, and that's okay as well. If you saw this book and picked it up, it's because you are different. You want the life that few are living. You want the opportunities, the lifestyle, and the freedom of a six-figure income. There's nothing wrong with wanting that. Don't ever let anyone make you feel bad for wanting what's best. When you're at your best, it allows you to perform at your best and help those around you. You are on your way!

WHAT ARE HABITS?

What are habits? Habits are subconscious decisions you make daily that make up your life and everyday actions. When I say subconscious decisions, I mean decisions you don't even know you're making most of the time. Like brushing your teeth, taking a shower, drinking your coffee, getting dressed, driving to work, eating food, watching TV shows, biting your nails, spending money, going to the gym, and anything else you do regularly without really thinking about it. It's basically your life routine. Habits can change and form at any time, depending on the circumstances and environment. Habits can either make you, break you, build you up, or keep you content and comfortable. The last thing you want to do is become comfortable. It kills dreams and goals. Humans, by default, want to be comfortable. We want easy and pain-free. To be successful in anything, you must be the opposite. You need to get comfortable with being uncomfortable in life and business. I'm not talking about anomalies; I'm talking about in general.

Successful people have better habits than most. When I say better, I mean better in terms of moving one step closer to becoming the best version of themselves. They have learned that the better one's habits, the more successful one can become and the easier success is. Habits are habits. They don't care if they are helpful or detrimental. If they are helping you or destroying you. If they are helping or killing the life of your dreams. Habits themselves have no choice in the matter; you have complete control of making your life filled with good habits or bad.

Take a look at your day from start to finish; what are your habits? If you're honest with yourself, do your current habits help you move closer to your goals or further away? For example, if your goal is to lose twenty pounds before summer, would your habit of beers every night with co-workers or your breakfast burrito on the

"Successful people are simply those with successful habits."

— BRIAN TRACY

way to work help you to reach your goal? These activities are clear NOs! You should know this. It's very common knowledge, and you should know that changing these two habits would get you closer to your goal. Most habits are easy to identify as beneficial or detrimental towards your goals or life in general. Everyone knows a piece of fruit is better for your health and overall being than a candy bar. Everyone knows that drinking water is better for you than drinking soda. Everyone knows that reading a book in your field of interest or profession is better for your future than watching old reruns of a TV show. The list goes on and on with examples of what we know is good for us and what we know is bad. So why do we see the difference and still choose the bad? Why would we knowingly do things that are detrimental to our success and move us farther away from our goals? The answer is simple; they're easy. (For more on habits and a simple formula for forming good habits, see Appendix D: Habits Can Be Good or Bad.)

> **PRO TIP:** *Write your goals down every day!* ***Every day!***

HABITS AND GOALS

The ultimate goal is to create and insert habits into our lives that move us closer to our goals and makes our lives easier and more enjoyable. When our lives are more enjoyable, those around us experience a more enjoyable version of you. People want to spend time with you and refer business to you. You experience less stress and make better decisions based on your client's needs, not your own. You are controlling your day instead of your day controlling you. That's the key to winning—total control of your time and your schedule. Discipline and habits are two areas in your life that you must work on every day and learn to control.

DISCIPLINE AND HABITS

You can apply the same principles to every area and aspect of your life. Using discipline to form your new habits and let go of your old habits plays a major role in your success. There are areas in your life that you are probably more disciplined than you realize. It may show up in eating, working, drinking, working out, hanging out with friends, hobbies, relationships, religion, memberships, and anything else that requires discipline. When you are monitoring your days, pay attention to the areas where you have forced discipline already. Why do you have discipline in some areas and not others? Will you let someone down? Will you pay a fine or fee? Are there consequences? There's a reason, and you must find it. Once you realize what that reason is, learn to find a motive in the new habits you want to form—a why will move you and force discipline. You will thank me later. The benefits and rewards of good discipline and habits will show up and amaze you. You're welcome.

3 ACTION STEPS

1. Choose three areas in your life you want to improve (business, fitness, diet, etcetera).
2. Choose three habits you want to lose and three habits you want to gain.
3. Start applying your discipline to all six areas. Begin with small steps, and apply the Kaizen Way technique.

"Formal education will make you a living; self-education will make you a fortune."

– JIM ROHN

CHAPTER 3

PERSONAL DEVELOPMENT AND GROWTH

Improve Every Day in Every Way

Let's start with a scenario. Say there were five people stuck on a deserted island, and all they had was each other, their minds, talents, abilities, and materials that the island contained. Now let's say the five people included: a farmer, a contractor, a doctor, a chef, and the last guy doesn't have a job, nor has he ever. The fifth guy lives off a trust fund and plays video games all day from his sofa.

Which person would you say carries the least value in the above situation? I'm not talking about as a human; I'm talking about from a utilitarian aspect: a survival position. I'm assuming most people would choose the last person, the jobless person that lived off a trust. However, this means we assume they all have the same attitudes, personalities, and physical capabilities. If the doctor was a dick then he would probably be found the least useful. I'm kidding, but do you see my point? Your skills and talents play a significant role when it comes to your position in society. The more you learn and grow as a human, the more valuable you are to society. You can solve more problems than most. Your brain and mind can solve more complicated problems than the next person. You can connect dots when most can't. You can formulate a clear sense of what needs to get done in the current situation. The more value you bring to society, the more the people will pay you. This is why it is extremely important to become obsessed with personal growth in all areas. Everything you learn either teaches you what to do or what not to do. People will notice. You will notice. It's so worth it.

How valuable do you think you are to society? If you had to put a value on all your skills, mentality, and ability to help people on a scale of 1 to 10, where would you rate yourself? Do you have a high school education? Do you have some college education or a degree? Do you have any real estate designations? Do you have any certifications? How many books have you read? How many seminars have you attended? How many podcasts have you listened to that have helped you grow as a person? How much experience do you have? Would you hire you? Elon Musk said, and I believe, "You get paid in direct proportion to the value you give and the problems you can solve." This is so true and obvious in society. Now I'm not saying one life is more valuable than another; what I'm saying is your mind is more beneficial to society, or less helpful to society based on how much you've learned and experienced through life.

Even when you look at the traditional, formal education system, the more schooling you have in a given field, the more you get paid. Someone with only a high school diploma will typically get paid less than someone with a bachelor's degree, and the master's degree typically does better than the bachelor's degree, and the

"The more you learn, the more you earn."

— WARREN BUFFET

PhD typically gets paid the most. I'm not speaking about anomalies either like Steve Jobs, Elon Musk, Richard Branson, or any other super-wealthy person that didn't attend or complete formal education. I'm talking about the majority of society and the basic structuring of modern society.

I like to use the analogy of buying a computer from the store. When you first buy a computer, take it out of the box, and plug it in; it may have a couple of programs or software on it. And what do you typically do to make it more useful for you and the projects that you want to accomplish? You buy software, and you upload it onto your computer to make your computer more powerful and more useful. Imagine if you had the choice to buy one computer that was fresh out of the box or to buy a computer that had every software program downloaded onto it for the exact purposes you need. You would probably pay more for the computer that has everything already on it. Essentially, you're a computer from birth that has a few programs on it—eating, sleeping, going to the bathroom, the ability to learn, etcetera. As you move through life, you accumulate programs and download software into your brain and mind that will either help you, cause you harm, help you grow, help you help others, allow you to get a particular job or career, perform activities, control your diet and exercise, solve problems and help you fit or stand out in society. Tony Robbins says, "Progress is the key to happiness." Progress is moving forward. Always becoming the best version of yourself every day in every way. Grow, Grow, Grow!

Most people stop growing and learning or drastically slow down after high school or after any formal education they've received that will allow them to get a job to pay the bills. They stop reading. They stop going to seminars. They basically stop learning and growing. They become content, complacent, and comfortable with where they are and who they are. There's nothing wrong with that. It's perfectly okay if that's your goal. Now, if you complain about where you're at in life and want a better life for yourself, your family, and those around you, you must become more valuable. The more valuable you are to society, the more people you can help and problems you can solve. The result is that you will get paid more. Don't believe me? Take a look around.

Look at the people who are where you want to be in life. Look at people you admire. Put that name into YouTube and watch as many videos as you can about that person. More than likely, they will mention how they are constantly learning and growing in their field. They are obsessed with absorbing information to become the best daily. To stand out. They had mentors and learned from them. They constantly seek out the latest and greatest information to give them the edge over their competition. Talent can only get you so far. Work and growth are vital to reaching the pinnacle in anything worth achieving.

Designations are a way for you to prove your value and show your quest for continued professional improvement. Designations are additional certifications you can acquire by attending either an online or classroom course, passing a test, and paying the fees and costs associated with the designation. I currently have seven designations and have no intention of stopping anytime soon. Additionally, I'm a licensed broker. I believe all education and designations are important because they are specialized for your field, real estate. (For more information on designations, see Appendix E: Designations Help You Prove Your Value.)

The way I look at it is even if you get only one solid new idea that changes the way you do business, that improves what you already do, or that gets you one deal, it's worth it. Plus, you have the information now, and nobody can take that from you. It's a win-win situation. In 2008, when the real estate market crashed, only the strong survived, and I'm not just talking about home buyers and sellers; I'm speaking of the real estate agents. If you didn't have experience in distressed sales, you were lost. Everyone was speaking a new language that only experienced agents knew and understood. I had to take a step back and reevaluate my career and the current market. What I realized was I needed to learn everything I could about distressed sales. I researched and found two designations related to short sales and foreclosures, Short Sales and Foreclosure Resource (SFR) and Distressed Properties Professional (DPP). These designations were game-changers for me and saved my real estate career. I went on to learn the processes and procedures of a short sale, how to work them, and how to educate my clients. I learned the foreclosure process as well. It was so crucial because I learned the schematics, how to communicate with the people in hardships, what their options and solutions were, and how to get them out of the bad situation and on with their lives. When you know what people are going through and fully understand their situation, you can put yourself in their shoes and show empathy.

It was actually a twofer deal: I turned over a leaf to a whole new area of real estate that would allow me to continue selling homes, and it allowed me to help homeowners who were under water and needed help. Homeowners who needed direction. They needed someone to navigate them through these times of uncertainty and help them put their lives back in order. I became that person. It was great.

Another designation that a few guys on my team have received is the Military Relocation Professional (MRP) because San Diego is one of the largest military towns in the world. It makes sense to learn how to communicate with these homebuyers who are looking to take advantage of their Veteran Affairs (VA) home loan. If I had the time to tell you how many deals they have closed, I would, but I don't; so let's just say a lot. The point is that designations work, and they are worth the investment in yourself. (For a list of twenty

PERSONAL DEVELOPMENT AND GROWTH

different real estate designations offered, see Appendix E: Designations Help You Prove Your Value.)

Seminars are another great way to not only learn new skills and get motivated, but you can also meet great people and make valuable connections while attending. While some people just attend seminars to attend, you need to be very intentional. Go on your local REALTOR® association website and take a glance at the seminars they have coming up. Identify the ones that cover an area that you want to learn more about and reserve the time to go.

There are also many real estate trainers, including myself, that hold multi-day seminars that go deep on an advanced topic. At these seminars, there are typically a few different speakers, great energy, and an environment dialed in for success and learning. Attend as many as possible. Do not feel guilty spending money on anything that will give you a deeper understanding and add to your abilities.

Anything you learn adds to your knowledge toolbox. Everything new you learn gives you a one-up on anyone that doesn't have the information you know. The great news, no one can take that from you. You never know when you will need any piece of knowledge you gain over time. Read as much as you can. Attend as many seminars as you can. Watch as many educational videos as you can. Talk to as many mentors as you can. Take them to lunch. Hire a coach as soon as you can. Experience as much as you can, and travel as much as you can. Do as much as you can do with where you are right now. It all adds up to a richer experience and a better lifestyle. I tell agents the best thing you can do is build rapport with not just your database but also with anyone and everyone you come in contact. You never know when you may come across them again and need a favor.

Real estate is a numbers game, so network with as many people as possible and learn as much as possible, so you have data points to connect. Every connection counts. The more personal, the better. The deeper, the better. I tell my agents all the time, you may know

"Rapport is the ability to enter someone else's world, to make them feel that you understand him, that you have a strong common bond."

— TONY ROBBINS

PERSONAL DEVELOPMENT AND GROWTH

everything about real estate in the world, but if a client is interviewing several agents and the client's child went to the same school as one of the interviewing agent's kids, you may lose. This is rapport. People want that connection. Humans are social creatures that crave acceptance. People want to work with people they like and who are like themselves. Build rapport. All the time in every way. Be aware of yourself and your environment at all times and look for ways to constantly find those connection points. The smallest connection point could potentially be the difference between you getting the client or your competitor getting the client. Rapport is powerful. Learn it. Use it.

Here is a graph showing you the level of education one has compared to their salary over a lifetime. This is formal education's viewpoint that is comparing different levels of education based on degrees earned from traditional colleges and universities. It's hard to determine how many books read is equal to income, so I used formal education. This graph would be even more powerful

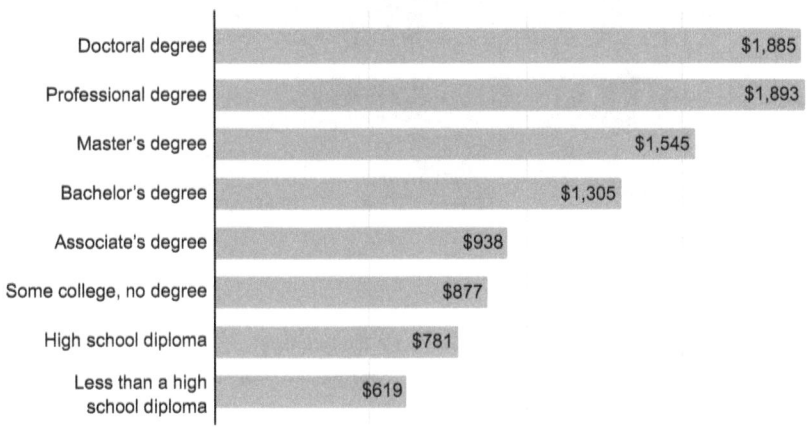

Note: Data are for persons age twenty-five and over. Earnings are for full-time wage and salary workers.
Source: Current Population Survey, U.S. Department of Labor, U.S. Bureau of Labor Statistics.
https://www.bls.gov/emp/chart-unemployment-earnings-education.htm

6 FIGURES IN 12 MONTHS

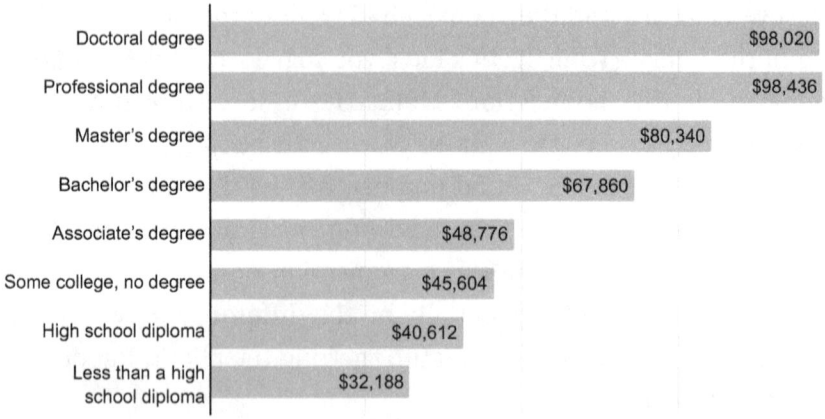

Note: Data are for persons age twenty-five and over. Earnings are for full-time wage and salary workers.
Source: Current Population Survey, U.S. Department of Labor, U.S. Bureau of Labor Statistics.
https://www.bls.gov/emp/chart-unemployment-earnings-education.htm

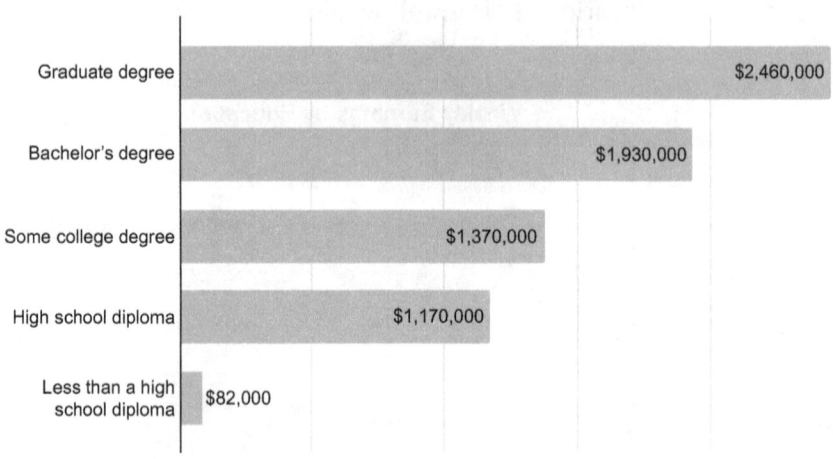

Source: Education and Lifetime Earnings. Social Security Administration.
https://www.ssa.gov/policy/docs/research-summaries/education-earnings.html

if you compared it to someone that reads books every day and is self-taught. The point I'm making is the more you learn, the more you earn.

As you can see, the more formal education one has, the more that person will make over a lifetime. And it's not peanuts. It's a lot of money, especially between the people with no education versus professional degrees. It's literally a completely different life. No matter what's important to you, more money can always help.

This chart is basically only taking into consideration the traditional degrees and education. At the top of the pyramid are the people that not only have a base of information and knowledge, but these are also the people that are lifelong learners. They invest into themselves more than any other investment. Warren Buffet, Bill Gates, and Elon Musk were the first people I remember pushing massive learning, besides my teachers in school.

Warren Buffet spends 5–6 hours a day reading. He was known in his prime to read upwards of 1000 pages a day. Now since he is slowing down a little, he only reads 500 pages per day. Crazy right? I'm up to 120–130 pages per day as I write this, and it's challenging. I can say that it does get easier the more you read. When I first started reading, I could only read five to ten pages and be done. Eyes and brain would hurt. I would begin to forget what I was reading and would have to re-read the page again. I remember thinking, there is no way someone is reading 500 pages a day or a book a day. It's impossible. I was wrong. Over the years, I have read about and met people that read a book a day. It can be done.

Bill Gates takes a two-week "reading" trip once a year. He runs off for two weeks with a bunch of books and reads the entire time. Elon Musk read every book in the library from the town where he grew up. He then moved because there were no more books to read. Elon Musk basically self-taught himself how to build rockets. Yes!

These men are three of the wealthiest people in the world, and they read and learn non-stop. They publicly admit to their constant learning and obsessive curiosity for everything. That's all I needed to hear. If you want to become successful, the quickest way is to emulate those who are already successful and in a place you want to be. The richest and most successful have been saying this for years. It's a simple formula. The more you know, the more dots you can connect, and the more people you can help. People pay large amounts of money to other people who can solve their problems or make life easier. It's always seemed pretty straightforward to me.

3 ACTION STEPS

1. Identify the designations that will be best for your area. Schedule time to take the classes required to achieve these certifications.
2. Subscribe to three YouTube channels for motivation and learning. Examples: TED Talk, Tom Bilyeu, and Ed Mylett.
3. Do a deep dive into a successful (and famous) person you admire. Read his/her biography and sign up for his/her newsletter, if available.

CHAPTER 4

TIME MANAGEMENT AND TIME BLOCKING

That Which Gets Measured Gets Done

How does your calendar look? What is your schedule? Are you good with time? Are you the person who is always early, always late, or always on time? Do you make excuses that you're always late and you've always been like that? Is that your self-talk? How do you feel when someone is late to meet you? Do you find yourself running from appointment to appointment with no time to spare and becoming stressed out? Do you find that you never have enough time to complete the necessary action items because you don't have enough time? Do you catch yourself saying, "I wish there were more hours in the day" or "I wish I could clone myself so I could get everything done?" The sad thing is you've probably dreamed about these impossibilities more than once.

"All time management begins with planning."

– TOM GREENING

TIME MANAGEMENT AND TIME BLOCKING

A common saying is that if you're on time, you are already late, but if you're early, you're on time. I believe this statement to be true. The most valuable commodity we possess is time. More than money. Once we spend it, there's no getting it back. It is gone forever. So why don't we understand time and its value? Why don't we use our time more wisely? Imagine if you knew exactly when you were going to die. Would you act differently? Would you spend your time differently and with other people doing things you have always wanted to do?

We have clocks and watches everywhere, yet many people can't seem to get a grip on time. Now, if you're one of those people who is always on time and punctual, good for you. You're a step ahead of the crowd. For the rest of you, the first thing you need to do is learn how to be on time and be aware of it. Admitting the problem is the first step. No justifications. No excuses. Admit you are terrible with time, so you can start working on fixing it. Second, you need to make sure you are using your time wisely and efficiently, especially to reach the goals required to set up the life you want and deserve. Time management and time blocking are key elements to your real estate success if you're going to sell at a high level, the level that will make you six figures.

Time Management refers to how you organize, plan, and spend your time on specific activities to maximize efficiency. Do you know any high-performing, high-producing real estate agents that are not good with time? It's rare. Most agents of this caliber organize and manage their time to the minute. It may be a calendar, an assistant, a schedule they keep, or an internal clock that they have mastered. If you sit down with one of these high-performers and ask about their time and schedule, they will typically answer fairly quickly and have a plan in place. They will also more than likely explain how they haven't always been the best with time until they started to get so busy it was forced upon them.

Real estate is a very consumable business regarding time so not having a grip on your time is a sure way to fail, or worse, be mediocre. Real estate is a demanding career, so in my opinion, mediocre is not an option. We deal with way too much stress working as hard as we do *not* to make six figures. The good news is that with some hard work and applied discipline, anyone can become better, if not great, with their time.

Where do you fit in as far as time on a scale of 1 to 10, with 1 being terrible and 10 being perfect? Be honest, that's the only way we can make progress. Are you saying to yourself, "I'm terrible with time, and I thought real estate was flexible and allowed me to make my own schedule?" This is very true. Real estate is so flexible that you don't even have to show up to the office, and no one will check in with you. No one will call and fire you for not showing up or doing your job. It sounds great until your bills come in and you can't pay them. One of the biggest mistakes I see in new and seasoned agents who aren't consistently producing is mismanaging their schedules. They don't track their time and activities and wake up at the end of the month with no homes sold and no active buyers or sellers.

When I ask them to scrutinize their day to see what happened, the truth comes out. They were side-tracked with a family member. They had to get their brakes fixed on their vehicle. They had to go to the department of motor vehicles. Their dog wasn't feeling well, and they didn't want to leave it alone. They had to wait for the Internet guy to come to the house. They confused networking to get clients with happy hour to have fun, and blah blah blah. The excuses come flying out. If this is you, don't worry; you're not alone, and you can improve.

Most people get into real estate from a 9-to-5 job or a forty- to fifty-hour workweek. If they were to dedicate the same hours in real estate and treat their new career like they did their last job in terms of scheduling, they would increase their probability of success. I tell agents all the time that they just need to work the same schedule as they did at their previous job. The same hours. Replace the activities of their last job with the real estate activities in this book.

What I've learned is it's a lot easier said than done. After selling real estate as a broker for over sixteen years, this trend is way too common. The truth of the matter is if you're lucky, the freedom comes eventually after all the hard work. The freedom comes from having control of your day, meaning completing all business activities and working your ass off consistently. When you do the right things for a long enough time, you get very efficient with your time and activities. The more efficient you become, the more results you will start to experience. The more efficient you become, the more free time you will have. If you don't do this, you will always feel rushed and under the gun. You will always feel like there's not enough time in the day. You will always wonder how the agents making six figures do it.

Another reason time management and time blocking are so necessary while working toward six figures and beyond is because once you get a few sales going, it's very easy to get caught up babysitting the deal to make sure it closes. This is one of the biggest mistakes an agent can make. I see this mistake hindering careers and holding people back from having breakthroughs. What do I mean? When you don't use time blocks, it's easy to forget to do the activities that you did to get you the deals you currently have. Example: You get three homes in escrow. The week before, you went to the office, made an educational video to post on social, sent out ten notecards, made your calls and texts, and had three coffee appointments. Great job! The three escrows pop the following week. You come in Monday, and instead of doing the activities just listed that got you the three escrows, you decide to schedule home inspections, go over disclosures, show your clients friends and family the home, and spend countless hours making sure every little detail is covered in your transaction. Congratulations, you are setting yourself up for failure. What should you do? You should **KEEP** the schedule you had prior to getting your deals under contract. Those activities should be an appointment with yourself. Do not deviate.

I hear you saying, "But Jeff, my clients could only do the inspection in the morning." Wrong answer. You tell your client you have an appointment already scheduled for that time and day, but you can meet them after lunch. Keep your mornings, from 9am to 12pm, open only to cater to your database and to produce and post content. This will be extremely hard at first. I know because I went through it, and I see countless numbers of agents still going through it. I get it; you need the money. You need those deals to close. I can assure you that everyone will wait for your available times. This is a great secret that no one can seem to figure out. Most agents get two to three deals in their pipelines and freeze up. They wonder why they can't get past that number of sales at one time. This is the secret. Keep doing the activities. This is how you break through.

When I learned this, I went from carrying four to five escrows to eight to eleven escrows at a time. It was a complete game-changer when I made the shift. I was once told by a coach and friend, Ashley Lunn of Keller Williams, always remember multiple people are working the deal: two agents, two transaction coordinators, a title rep, an escrow officer and their assistant, and a lender and their assistant and processors. If they need you for something, they will let you know. It will go through all those people first until it's an emergency. This was the best advice I've ever received as far as working a deal. There will be emergencies you must attend to, I get it. Be very picky and determine what can wait or what needs to get done asap. Let everyone do their job so you can get back to selling homes, which is your job. I'm not saying to let the deal go

TIME MANAGEMENT AND TIME BLOCKING

and completely forget about it; I'm saying use time blocks to schedule time to work the deal. Very simple, but not easy.

Now that we know why time management is essential to your success let's discuss the other side, time blocking. What is time blocking? I know I keep mentioning it, so now I'll explain it. **Time blocking** is a method used for aggressive productivity by scheduling every hour of your day. Time blocking bundles blocks of time together to perform a particular task or action throughout the day. Every minute of the day is accounted either for work or personal. You schedule everything, and you don't deviate from the plan. No matter what.

I encourage you to make your own calendar based on your business. You can put it right in your Google calendar and set up alarms for reminders. Stick to this plan. Do not deviate. This is one of the most critical pieces to a six-figure business. (For a simple example

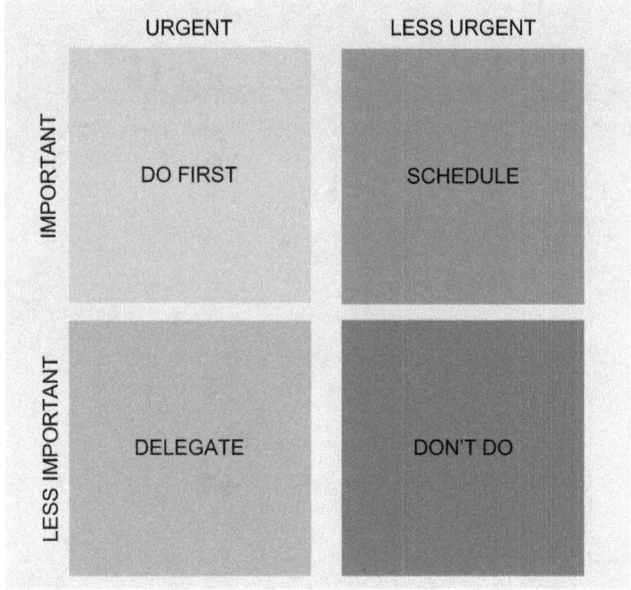

*Here is a quadrant to help you determine which tasks you should do yourself and which tasks you should delegate. **ALWAYS** do the Urgent/Important first.*

"You either make yourself accountable or you will be made accountable by your circumstances."

– UNKNOWN

of how a successful real estate calendar looks with proper time blocking, see Appendix F: Manage Your Week to Win the Year.)

Let's talk about the other piece of the time management and time blocking puzzle: **Accountability.** Having the perfect dialed-in and time blocked real estate calendar is great but means nothing if you don't follow and execute it. One way to automate this is to use an online calendar for scheduling. You don't have to share the link with clients if it feels like you are giving them personal information. You can pull it up yourself and enter their information to confirm a time. Goals without action and time set aside for execution are only dreams. We must set up a plan to execute our goals and then take massive action. That's where most people fail. They have huge dreams and even get as far and planning out how they will accomplish them but fail to take the proper action.

Most people get paralysis by analysis when it comes to putting their goals and dreams into action. Some sort of accountability is a mandatory trait one must have to reach the pinnacle of success and become part of the 1 percent.

Personal accountability is the hardest. We know we want to do something, and we plan it. We get excited, start doing research and discover exactly what it will take to accomplish the feat at hand, and then BOOM, nothing. They end up with lots of forgotten dreams due to a lack of self-accountability and self-discipline. Let's take another example, the gym: you look in the mirror and notice those extra twenty pounds you've put on over the years. You feel it. You know you can feel better if you made a few small changes to your diet and physical activity. You drive down to the local gym and sign up for a membership, head to the local mall and pick up some new workout gear and shoes, and you're on your way to a healthy lifestyle.

The next morning you wake up, and...you overslept. It's ok; you'll start tomorrow. The following day, you actually get up and get dressed to go to the gym. You get to the gym and walk in only to find yourself too nervous and embarrassed to try any machines. You know what you need to do. Just start. But you don't. You tell yourself it was a good first day at the gym and head home. This happens a few more days, and slowly but surely, you stop going altogether and justifying it with some lame excuse. That is a lack of self-accountability and discipline. Take control of that little voice in your head and make it follow orders. You're in control. Self-accountability is a muscle that's definitely worth building.

Public accountability is when you ask others to hold you accountable for your goals and actions. My example is checking in on social media when I go to the gym. People give me shit for it all the time. Doesn't bother me. I put it out there so when people see me not checking in, they ask if I've stopped working out. That's one way of using the public as an accountability partner.

Let's look at accountability in other ways. Say you want to arrange an open house every day for a month. Post a video letting all your followers know that you will be holding an open house every day for a month. You would also tell them that you will be posting or going live from the open house on social media. Let them know they are more than welcome to stop by and check out the house. Consciously or subconsciously, you will wake up every day and do an open house because you will know there's a possibility someone may show up, and someone will be expecting a video of your open house that day. In fact, there is an excellent chance someone will let you know if you miss a day. It's a psychological trick you can play on yourself. You can also have competitions with friends for the same goal, and the loser has to pay up. If it's fitness, the goal could be the first person to be able to do fifty push-ups in a row, or the one who comes in first out of your group in the marathon coming up in three months, or the first person to get a six-pack. You set the goals. This type of friendly competition works between friends, family, and co-workers. We use it all the time around the office in a productive, positive way.

When it comes to real estate, daily accountability will determine your success. I know this because I've seen it all. I've seen agents fail, and I've seen them get rookie of the year. I paid attention. I looked for the traits of the ones that became successful. Accountability of their days, weeks, and months was massive. The days turn to weeks. The weeks turn to months, and the months turn to years. One thing I know because I have felt it myself, and others have told me the same thing: Time flies. Think back five years ago, say the year out loud and watch all the memories pop up in your mind. Doesn't it feel like yesterday? Think back ten years. Can you think of a few events? It really doesn't seem that long ago, does it? We all have the same amount of time in a day. How come some people are better off than others at managing it and become more successful while others never seem to reach their goals? **ACCOUNTABILITY!**

When you sit down and lead-generate, you open your customer relationship manager (CRM) and have your accountability form out on your desk. Your accountability form is your tool you use to stay on-track with your monthly and weekly goals and contains fields for you to enter information such as the phone, text message, and in-person contacts you made for the week; the business cards you handed out; the contact information of any new names you need to add to your database; and social media messaging that occurred. As you go through your CRM and make connections, you record them in your CRM and write the name in the blank on the form. I know some of you are balking at the idea of paper or using a form when you have technology to get the job done. I get it. It sounds a little old school. Please just do this. It's a major form of accountability, and because you're recording it in two separate sources, it feels twice as good. It feels like an accomplishment and releases a little dopamine each time you write a new name in that form and check it off as a connection for the day. (For the weekly accountability forms we use at Discher Group, see Appendix G: Leverage Accountability to Become Successful Faster.)

Remember, real estate is a numbers game. The more people you speak with, the higher the probability of you getting a new client. Stick to this exercise of filling out this form weekly for a year. This form should accompany you through your three hours of lead generation each day. If you fill out the accountability form completely, then you will have more business than you will know what to do with every week. Start filling it out ASAP. If it doesn't work, email me at Jeff@DischerGroup.com, and I'll refund your money for this book. **BOOM!**

3 ACTION STEPS

1. Set up your schedule by time blocking your week, so it's aligned with your goals.
2. Put your time-blocked calendar in your phone and make sure it's synced with your laptop, computer, and tablet. The more you see it, the better.
3. Create the weekly accountability form found in Appendix G: Leverage Accountability to Become Successful Faster, and print out fifty-two copies of it, one for each week of the year.

SUMMARY

The best way to improve your chances of success in any industry is to train your mind to do the tasks necessary to achieve greatness. In real estate, you will be competing with the part-time and inexperienced agents who think that a license is enough to be a good agent.

Do the inner work to ready your mind, and you will outshine the majority in the field.

The way you start the day can tell you a lot about your potential for success. Start working while other people are still dreaming, and you will advance faster than your peers. Morning rituals are the building blocks to a thriving life that keeps you happy and healthy enough to work toward achieving your goals.

James Clear said it best, "Habits are not a finish line to be crossed, they are a lifestyle to be lived." You need to establish the morning rituals and habits that a six-figure real estate agent would embody. Successful people have better habits than most. When I say better, I mean better in moving one step closer to becoming the best version of themselves. They have learned that the better their habits are, the more successful they can become, and the easier it is to achieve the goals they have in mind. Use incremental successes to continue to raise the bar of your habits and behaviors.

Look at the people that are where you want to be in life. Put their name into the YouTube search bar and watch as many videos as you can about that person. More than likely, they will mention how they are constantly learning and growing in their field. They are obsessed with absorbing information to become the best daily. They are continually seeking out the latest and greatest information to give them the edge over their competition because talent can only get you so far. Work and personal growth are vital to reaching the pinnacle in anything worth achieving.

Designations are a way for you to prove your value and show your quest for continued professional improvement. Designations are additional certifications you can acquire by attending either an online or classroom course, passing a test, and paying the fees and costs associated with the designation. (For more information on designations, see Appendix E: Designations Help You Prove Your Value.)

Learn everything you can, real estate and beyond, so that you can connect with people on multiple levels. Experience as much as you can, and travel as much as you can. Do as much as you can do with where you are right now. It all adds up to a richer experience and a better lifestyle. I tell agents all the time, the best thing you can do is build rapport with not just your database, but with anyone and everyone. You never know when you may come across them again and need a favor.

Time management and time blocking are critical elements to your real estate success. Especially if you want to sell at a high level, the level that will make you six figures.

Time Management refers to how you organize, plan, and spend your time on specific activities to maximize efficiency. High-performing and high-caliber real estate agents succeed in business because they manage their time to the minute. It may be a calendar, an assistant, a schedule they keep, or an internal clock that they have mastered. If you sit down with one of these high performers and ask about their time and schedule, they will typically answer fairly quickly and have a plan in place. They will also more than likely explain how they haven't always been the best with time until they started to get so busy it was forced upon them.

The beginning of your real estate career is the perfect time—Did you see what I did there?!—to implement a structured schedule that will ready your mind and your day for success. Time blocking and time management are so necessary while working to get to six figures and beyond because once you get a few sales going, it's very easy to get caught up focusing on the wrong aspects of the transaction.

When it comes to real estate, daily accountability will determine your success. Personal accountability is the most likely to fail so instead of counting on yourself to do the right thing every time, build public accountability with your team or share with your audience on social media when and where they can expect to see you next.

In the following section of the book, you will build on the mental skills you have learned and discover how to Build Strong Business Foundations.

BUILD STRONG
BUSINESS
FOUNDATIONS

"K.I.S.S. Keep It Simple Stupid"

– KELLY JOHNSON

CHAPTER 5

FOCUS POINTS OF BUSINESS

Go All-In on Three Activities

Real estate is a very simple business; it's just not an easy business. I've been selling real estate and training people for more than seventeen years, and I've seen it all. I've worked at multiple offices, worked with hundreds of agents, coached and mentored agents, worked in leadership, and sold hundreds of homes as a real estate broker.

I remember when I started my career in 2004, and the company had training for new agents. They would give you twenty to thirty different lead-generating activities and say "Get to work." They threw everything, including the kitchen sink, at me; it was only years later that I realized every other agent was just as confused as I was as to where to start.

Do I do open houses? If so, how often? How do I find sellers? What's the protocol? Do I call For Sale by Owners (FSBOs)? Where do I get the names and numbers for these people? Do I contact bankruptcy attorneys? Do I call divorce attorneys? What do I say if they answer? Do I pick five hundred homes and start mailing to them every month? And if so, what do I send them? Again, where do I get the names and phone numbers for these people? Do I pick a neighborhood and start knocking on doors? How do I choose a neighborhood? How many communities do I choose? Do I post on social media? If so, what platforms and how often? These are all questions I had, and knowing where to start continues to be one of the top challenges for new agents.

I HEARD ALL THE FRUSTRATIONS when I was at a couple of the larger brokerages with hundreds of agents. I listened and compared what people were saying to what I was experiencing in my business. Agents get overwhelmed with choosing what to do, how to start, and where to start. It's like eating at Cheesecake Factory and trying to choose what to order off a menu that has 2,000 options. There's a real name for having too many options to choose from; it's called **choice overload**. (Alvin Toffler first introduced the term in his 1970 book, *Future Shock*.) If we can barely choose our clothes to wear in the morning, how are we supposed to decide how and what to do to start our real estate career? Very confusing, and very real paralysis by analysis.

What I've learned after trying most strategies is simple—choose a maximum of three major tactics and maybe one or two as extras and stick to them. Master and become obsessed with the tactics. Choose to be the best at doing these. Stand out. Take the time to research as many tactics as possible before choosing. This is important. It will save you time upfront and get you started establishing yourself as an expert through the few tactics you have chosen. You want to make sure that you can see yourself running your business like this for years and change things up to adapt when necessary.

Find agents in your area who run a business the way you would want to run yours and set up a lunch that you pay for as soon as possible. Successful people have egos and love talking about themselves and their success. They will tell you exactly what they do and how they do it, and most of the time, they will also show you how. Call your favorite agent on the phone and ask them to lunch and let them know why you are inviting them, and the check is on you! You are a new agent in the area, you are excited to start your career, and you admire that person's business model. Give them a couple of compliments and ask them to lunch. You can take it a step further and stalk their Facebook page to see where they like to eat and invite them with that location in mind.

Do not—I repeat—**do not come unprepared.** Take the time to really think about what you want to ask. Have a plan. Out of respect for their time, keep the conversation under thirty minutes unless it organically goes longer. You want to be very present and take as many notes as possible. You can even record the conversation so you can listen to it later but only if the prospective mentor consents to this, of course. This could be the best time you will spend figuring out your plan. Real-life experience and wisdom from the source itself are better than any book or seminar.

Times and technology are constantly evolving. When I first started in the business, the trending lead generating tactics were:

- Billboards (very expensive)
- Cold calling expired listings
- Cold calling canceled listings
- Cold calling FSBO's
- Clubs
- Farming a neighborhood

- Flyering a neighborhood
- Focusing on one neighborhood
- Open houses
- Magazine ads (very expensive)
- Networking events
- Networking groups
- Neighborhood events
- Sending out mailers (snail mail)
- Showing up at attorneys and other real estate related vendors with goodies
- Word of mouth

That was in 2004. There was very little one could do without a decent budget, which no new real estate agent typically has when they start. There was really no social media, and the Internet was just used for emails. It was a big deal when the multiple listing service (MLS) was made digital. If you wanted to be on TV or in a commercial, it would cost thousands of dollars for the airtime and another $5,000 to $10,000 to produce the commercial. I know because I did it. I had commercials on the local news channel. Could you imagine?

So, what has changed?

Social media!

Social media has changed the way real estate is conducted. It has introduced an entirely new way of doing business and leveled the playing field. It has taken the average age of a realtor from fifty-five-years-old to thirty-five-years-old. It has taken the cost of advertising media down to a fraction of what it once was and made it accessible to anyone and everyone with a smartphone, laptop, or tablet with access to the Internet.

What does the advent of social media mean? It means you can produce your own TV show on your phone for next to nothing.

All it takes is some guts, a little creativity, and the knowledge to start recording. We'll dive deeper into the how and the what in the next chapter. What used to cost $5,000 per month to be on a TV commercial can now be done for free. Your job is to build your audience by creating and distributing creative, valuable content that your audience wants. By doing this, you become the trusted source in real estate. You become the authority.

TECHNOLOGY IS ALWAYS EVOLVING

Another significant change that continues to evolve year after year is technology. We have everything we need at our fingertips in today's world. No excuses. Don't have the answer? It's okay; Google does. Just one second, and it'll have that for you. We have customer relationship managers (CRMs), so there are no excuses for not being in front of your clients every month and delivering value while entertaining them. CRMs remind you of your clients' birthdays, anniversaries, kids' birthdays, home purchase anniversaries, and even the last time you spoke to them. What does all of this data do? It makes building rapport a lot easier and more convenient for you as an agent. It takes out the guesswork. The CRM literally tells you how to do your job in terms of staying in front of your database. In the past, there were Rolodexes and desk calendars. Not saying a spinning wheel of contacts won't work, just saying there's an easier and more efficient way in this day and age. Don't get stuck in the past, or someone living in the present will take your business. Efficiency is key!

My point is, with all of these great technological advances and inexpensive options to get your business out there, find the three things you want to use and go all in. Work with your broker or coach to help determine what tactics best fits your personality and will give you the best results based on your market. Once you identify your tactics, find the best ways to implement them and stick to them. It will all happen in divine timing. Keep going. The more you change what you're doing, the longer it will take to see results. It's okay to give yourself time and be patient. Things will constantly evolve. You will find your lane. Consistency is key.

For the sake of this book, I will be discussing the three main strategies we use at Discher Group to help brand new agents get their jumpstart to their first six figures. One of my goals when developing the vision for the team was that I wasn't a fan of rejection. The traditional style of knocking on doors (expect some nasty rejection), calling FSBOs (more rejection), calling expired listings (when sellers are already pissed their house didn't sell), cold calling neighborhoods looking for sellers (more rejection), cold calling renters (more rejection), and the list goes on.

I'm a high "i" on the DiSC behavior self-assessment tool with a default "D." When I drilled down into the meaning of those letters on the profile, it was me. It's fairly accurate. (See Appendix H: Using the DiSC Assessment to Up-level Your Business for more on the DiSC assessment and how to use it.) As an "i" or "Influencer," I'm not a fan of rejection. The truth is the top real estate professionals and top salespeople, in general, are high I's. Guess what! "I's" do not like rejection. Most coaches or trainers tell us, the more "no's" you get, the closer you are to a "yes." It's very true in logic, but I don't like it. Your pride and ego take a pounding, which is not good for a newer agent just starting in a highly competitive business. I've never had to do any high-rejection strategies to build a healthy real estate business that's fun and worth owning. I'd rather give massive value with content, build awesome relationships, and have buyers and sellers calling me instead of spending hours cold calling people who don't want to talk to me.

FOCUS POINTS OF BUSINESS

My three tactics and the ones I teach my agents to use at Discher Group are **Social Media; Open House;** and the most important, **Database.** We will cover each of these in the next few chapters.

Are you READY? Let's go!

3 ACTION STEPS

1. Identify the three focus points/tactics on which you want to focus.
2. Find three top-producing agents and take them to lunch at restaurants of their choice.
3. Decide how you will approach the three focus points you have chosen.

"We don't have a choice on whether we DO social media, the question is how well we Do it."

— ERIK QUALMAN

CHAPTER 6

SOCIAL MEDIA

Creative, Entertaining, Value-Focused

The world and real estate have changed drastically over the last twenty years. Social media popped up and took over our lives and has had a major impact on most industries. If you don't have a social media presence or aren't planning on having one, you will eventually suffer and lose to your more visible competitors. It would be like owning a horse and when cars came out, you said you weren't giving up your horse because cars would never last. How did that work out? Change is inevitable, so accept and adapt accordingly. You're either evolving and growing or staying the same and dying. I say this because if you are reading this and dreading social media, get over it. The faster you master it and get comfortable with it, the faster you can take advantage of this game-changer.

I'll admit, I was nervous and insecure when I first started using social media, especially when it comes to posting a personal picture or video of myself. I would make every excuse in the book about why I didn't have to or didn't want to post or create content. I was stuck in my old ways until I realized what was happening. I started listening to people who were crushing it on social media and making a lot of money while having fun. I would get excited, and then the old me would kick in and get insecure. This is totally normal.

I knew social media would work; I would listen to Gary Vaynerchuk say it over and over, "You must be pumping out massive content and preferably video!" He gave a keynote at a real estate conference at the beginning of 2020 and literally stood in front of the entire conference and said, "If you don't incorporate social media and videos into your business, you will eventually lose." That hit different than just watching him on YouTube, and what he was saying made way too much sense. I started paying attention to how much I was on my phone and realized that everyone else was too. I would be at dinner and realize everyone would be on their phone at the same time. What were they doing when they were on their phones? Social media. So, what would happen if, while they were on social media, one of my videos pops up while they happen to be considering buying a home? They click on my profile and realize I'm local and know my shit and direct message me. BOOM! This happens all day, every day. It works.

Are you feeling overwhelmed with the whole idea of social media?

Just START! It will be tough. You will think you look and sound like shit. This is okay as long as it doesn't stop you from taking action. There are famous actors like Johnny Depp who don't watch any of their own movies. He's not the only famous actor who has admitted to this, and again, these thoughts are very normal. So what do you do if you are scared, nervous, and insecure about posting? As the late Kobe Bryant would say, You **GET OVER IT!**

I heard a great quote with regard to doing videos:

"You are not better looking in person, so just do it."

– UNKNOWN AUTHOR

Every time you open one of your social media apps, you're basically walking into a networking event. Everything you post gets scrutinized by your followers—whether for good or bad. Each post is your opportunity to show your followers that you are an authority at what you do and you're the best choice for them to buy or sell a home. Do you treat it that way? Are you intentional about what you post?

Look at your social media accounts right now! Do they scream, "I am an obsessed, real estate professional. Hire me!" or are your posts just a bunch of smiling cat photos? Now I'm not saying to be an annoying salesman; I'm saying that with the right post and message, your followers will categorize you as the real estate professional with authority or just one of their friends. You want BOTH. More than likely, your followers know at least five or ten other realtors on their feeds. **YOU** want to be the one they think of when they think "real estate." There's a WAY!

I get excited about social media, and I hope to get you excited as well. It's a fun way to be creative and entertaining while educating your followers. Have fun. Add your own style. Make it your own and make it stand out. How? By having a consistent strategy that follows some simple rules. Let's start with branding, which is the starting point of identifying who you are and what you do.

Everyone has a brand, whether they know it or not. Many people fail in business because they fail to brand themselves in a way that aligns with who they are and what they offer. One big mistake I see agents make is trying to be the "cool" guy or gal. They make it more about them than their audience. People can see right through someone trying to look cool instead of someone trying to give value. Every time you make a video, you need to consider to whom you're speaking and for what purpose. Are you speaking to help, add value, or teach your audience something new? Are you being vulnerable? That's the key with social media. Seek to understand

and then to be understood. Your brand and content should speak to your audience and give massive value while entertaining.

> **PRO TIP:** *Pay attention to the videos you like to watch on Facebook or YouTube to become aware of why you like them. Next time you come across a video you like, take note as to why you like it. Was it boring or entertaining? Was it short or long? Was it funny or serious? How did it sound? Was there music? Was there variation in the tonality of the voice? What was it that kept you watching? Take notes and reference them when you are creating content for yourself.*

CREATE THREE PILLARS OF CONTENT

Create three pillars of content to mix it up. These pillars should not only be your interests; they should be subjects that are part of your daily life. They should be topics that are always on your mind. Be consistent by posting every day. Give MASSIVE value by making branded videos showcasing your knowledge and providing easy-to-understand and applicable content to the problems your clients might have. Use stories to document your day as a realtor to show you're working. You can also use still photos to show who you are and also create a theme. I use positive quotes about business, success, finance, real estate, and fitness. Take a look at my Instagram profile, @isellrealestate. Do you see my pillars? Do you see my brand? Does it stand out? What can you do to make your social and brand scream who you are and what you do?

> **PRO TIP:** *Did you see my Instagram handle? Choose one for yourself that is something other than @NAMERealEstate. Make it*

> *something that will make your current clients look at you in a new way and that is one that potential clients won't have a hard time remembering.*

Identifying your three pillars for your social media presence is crucial, so the earlier you can do this step in your career, the better. Before learning the importance of this strategy, I would just post whatever, whenever. No research. No plan. No strategy. As you can imagine, that didn't work. I learned how to identify my three pillars from my friends at iLegendz Network, the branding experts. Visit their website iLegendz.com and check them out as well on all social media platforms. When you start closing deals, give them a call to take you to the next level. I am going to share with you what they share with me. It is their strategy on how to create a strong personal brand on social media. Let's look at the questionnaire below and get you started.

STEP 1: Creating Your Brand Image

What's your story? *Make sure you speak the truth and share your most vulnerable experience and how you came out of it in order to help others.*

_____

_____

_____

_____

_____

_____

What are your three brand pillars? What are the *categories that align with your content? Examples are travel, podcast host, real estate, fitness, mom life, dogs, cats, animals, piano, etcetera.*

1. _____

2. _____

3. _____

How will you help others? The goal of influence is to be an authority figure that others look up to for guidance, inspiration, motivation, and/or positivity.

_____

_____

_____

_____

_____

_____

STEP 2: Identify Your Target Audience

The best way to identify your target audience is to imagine your ideal follower. It helps to look at your audience analytics on social media to understand who's following now. (NOTE: It's critical that you envision an imaginary person, one who embodies every single trait that is indicative of who encompasses your whole audience.)

Is your ideal follower a male or female? M or F or Both

What's your ideal follower's main interest?
_____

Where do your ideal followers currently live?
_____

At which hashtags does your ideal follower look?
_____

In what stage of life is your ideal follower living? Examples: college, student, divorced, married, new baby, retired, traveler, etcetera.
_____

Complete this sentence with the above answers: My target person is a (gender) _____ aged (age range) _____, who lives in (city or state) _____ and who likes to (activity) _____.

STEP 3: Create and Distribute Content

Make content that supports your personal brand and is created with your ideal follower in mind. Be creative and entertaining. Show your unique expression through your content. The more often you post, the better your content gets. Consistency is KEY!

Document – We have phones on us every second of the day. That phone you have has a really good camera on it. Pull it out

> *"Your personal brand is another word for your reputation."*
>
> — MARCO CHAMPION

and start recording. Record what? Create videos of you working, showing property, at a home inspection, a party you're attending, maybe your workout or other daily activities, and anything else you want people to see. Make it authentic. Make it reflect your style and your daily routine.

Create – Tell a story. Educate. Have fun. Entertain.

Distribute – Get it out to the audience utilizing all social media platforms.

What is your pillar content? _____

What days of the week do you post each pillar?

_____

The times and days you post will change with the algorithm. You can Google the best times to post on each platform and get the most current times and dates. The algorithm changes frequently, so you have to stay on top of the most current times and days. Also, pay attention to when your clients are commenting and interacting the most. Check your insights. You will begin to notice when your best times to post are.

As you increase the frequency of your posts, keep in mind that hashtags are also important. Make sure you are utilizing the most current and trending hashtags in your market. An app called Hashtag Expert for iPhones will prove helpful in this endeavor. (Check other platforms such as Google Play to see if a similar app is available for other devices.) Hashtag Expert does all the legwork for you. You put in a topic, and it searches the Internet to see which hashtags are trending across the platforms the most for that subject.

SOCIAL MEDIA

You will notice more engagement and start to see more people begin to follow you. It works. Get it NOW!

STEP 4: Grow Your Audience

There are two ways to grow your audience. You either pay with **MONEY,** or you pay with **TIME. (The secret is to do both.)**

1. **Grow through collaboration:** This is done by teaming up with another influencer or person with followers you would want and collaborating with that person. The goal is to share each other's community and followers in hopes of exchanging audiences. Do a video together, interview the person you are collaborating with (they will share on their wall and possibly encourage their followers to check out your content), join a club or group to find people to collaborate with, such as Business Networking International (BNI) or Toastmasters. You can also tag people in the hopes that they will share your post. Again, this is all to build your followers and, ultimately, your database.
2. **Grow through networking:** This is the traditional way and still a solid method to grow your influence. Attend networking events and hand out your card or exchange contact information. Ask people directly for their social media handles and follow them right there on the spot. They will typically follow you back. Bonus tip: Take a selfie and tag them in it. This can be done in person or online. I tell my agents that you are entering a virtual networking event each time you log in to Facebook or Instagram. Take it a step further and look at Facebook Groups related to your field and start friending those people. DM people and send a personal note.

Example: *"Hey (insert name), Thanks for accepting my invitation and connecting. Your page looks awesome, and I see we have a few friends in common. I'm growing my database network of people like you that I already have something in common with and can't wait to get to know you better.*

How's your day?
Jeff"

3. **Grow through paid advertising:** This is pretty self-explanatory. Facebook, Instagram, YouTube, Google, and many other online platforms allow you to pay to play. It's actually the fastest way to grow your following. You tell these platforms what type of people you are looking to connect with, and they put your profile in front of as many of those types of people as you have the budget to acquire. You can get very specific when you run ads. If you don't know how to run ads, there are companies out there that can do it for you. If you don't have the money, keep growing organically until you can invest in the growth of your contacts. You can also research how you can create ads that work. YouTube has hundreds of videos that teach you step-by-step how to create ads. This is basically like running a TV commercial, but only people you want to see it will see it. Very efficient. Be patient. It will work.

The best thing you can do is do all three together. These platforms love when you spend money with them. The more you pay, the more people get to see what you are posting. It's business. The great thing is that you don't have to pay to start. Just start. Put out massive, value-giving content over time, and you will get noticed. Your content will also get better the more you do it. The more you get noticed, the more likely you are to build credibility and trust with your database. People want to work with people they like and trust, and this is the way to get to know and like people, and vice versa.

HOW OFTEN SHOULD I POST?

This is another question where people get stuck. They don't want to feel like they're posting too much. They don't want to feel like they're bothering their audience or annoying them. **NEWS FLASH:** Your audience doesn't care. If they think you're posting too much and block you or unfriend you, they wouldn't have sent you business anyway. That's the new function of your social business. The ideal depends on what platform you are posting on to start.

If you're using Facebook, you can post more because it's a rolling feed. Once you post something on Facebook, it's pretty hard to find a month later. It's gets buried fast. Instagram is stagnant, meaning someone can see all your post for the last year by looking at your page. I would only post once or twice per day on your page and thirty to forty times on your stories. YouTube is a library, so you can post as many videos on YouTube as possible. Ideally, you want to post on YouTube the same days and times each week. For example, Tuesdays and Thursdays at ten in the morning, or Monday, Wednesday, and Friday at noon. Every Saturday at 9 am. Still need some ideas to get you started on what to post? You should document your day and create content to educate and entertain your clients. Show them your day through stories. By stories, I mean storytelling, but the Instagram stories work, too. Show them you're working. It takes time to be aware and break out your phone all the time, but you will get used to it.

As of publication, these are the most recent days and times to post to maximize exposure and have the highest probability of having your post seen. But, again, these are always changing, so be sure to constantly check to see what's trending.

Best Time to Post on Facebook

- **Best Days** – Thursday, Friday, Saturday, and Sunday
- **Best Times** – 9:00 a.m. to 10:00 a.m. and 1:00 p.m. to 4:00 p.m.
- **Ideal Length of Characters for Post** – forty to eighty characters
- **Worst Day** – Tuesday
- Saturday and Sunday get the highest level of engagement on Facebook.

Best Time to Post on Instagram

- **Days** – Monday, Wednesday, and Thursday
- **Best Times** – 11:00 a.m. to 1:00 p.m. and 7:00 p.m. to 9:00 p.m.
- **Ideal Length of Characters for Post** – 138 to 150 characters
- **Worst Day** – Sunday
- Wednesday gets the highest level of engagement on Instagram.

Best Time to Post on Twitter

- **Best Days** – Monday, Tuesday, Wednesday, Thursday, and Friday
- **Best Times** – 8:00 a.m. to 10:00 a.m., noon to 1:00 p.m., and 4:00 p.m. to 6:00 p.m.
- **Ideal Length of Characters for Post** – seventy-one to one hundred characters
- **Worst Day** – Sunday
- Wednesday gets the highest level of engagement on Twitter.

Best Time to Post on LinkedIn

- **Best Days** – Tuesday, Wednesday, and Thursday
- **Best Times** – 9:00 a.m. to 11:00 a.m.

- Ideal Length of Characters for Post – fifty to one hundred characters
- Worst Day – Saturday and Sunday
- Wednesday gets the highest level of engagement on LinkedIn.

Best Time to Post on YouTube

- Best Days – Thursday, Friday, Saturday, and Sunday
- Best Times – 9:00 a.m. to 11:00 a.m. and noon to 4:00 p.m.
- Worst Day – Monday
- Saturday and Sunday get the highest level of engagement on YouTube.

VIDEO

Let's talk about video since I believe, along with other marketers, that it's the future of advertising for all businesses. Why does video work so well? Why are TV commercials some of the most expensive marketing out there? Yes, they are seen by a lot of eyes. I get it, but it's also the specific medium. Video tells a story. It allows the viewer to see the emotion and have emotion more than still photos, written words, or spoke language without images. When you have visual and audio together with emotion, it's powerful. That's why actors get paid the big bucks.

Now it's your turn. EVERYONE is scared. The key is to start. You don't even have to post the first videos you do. Make them in private. Edit them in private. If you feel like posting for your audience to see, then post. Keep making videos. Each one will get better. You will gain more confidence, and it will show through your videos. I tell every agent the same thing when they are hesitant to make and post a video; just be vulnerable and post your first video and watch what happens. You will get a bunch of likes and comments like, "Damn, you killed it! Good job!" It will feel good because it will confirm that video works to increase engagement. This will make you want to make more videos. Keep going! Keep making videos. People will get to know you for your videos. Start now while everyone is still scared. Grab your market share while it's available.

You are basically creating a real estate celebrity right in front of your audience. Imagine you and a friend go into a restaurant and sit down for lunch. You look over, and you see Bob, the weather guy you see on TV every morning before you leave the house. You whisper to your friend, hey, that's Bob, the weather guy from the morning news. Your friend may not know who he is, but you do, and you look over and say, "excuse me, you're Bob the weather guy, right?" and he smiles and says, "yes." You get a shot of dopamine because you just met a celebrity. You want to be Bob of real estate on social media. Anyone who watches TV is more than likely to be on social media just as often. Get in front of them! Become the authority that they will brag to their friends about meeting.

What the heck should I do videos about? That is the most frequent question I get asked by my agents. There are thousands of videos you could do. You can use the Lowest Common Denominators of real estate. Break the process down. Break a neighborhood down. Educate your audience and potential clients on any aspect of real estate. Get creative. Watch and listen to the market and pay attention to what's trending in the market, what issues buyers and sellers are seeing, and how you can prevent home buyers and sellers from making simple mistakes. I always recommend starting with simple real estate terms. It will help you learn them better while educating your audience. You can also create series, which you can plan out and that will keep you busy for weeks. Be intentional about topics and timing. Take your audience on a journey with you from start to finish of a transaction. Introduce them to your vendors and take advantage of borrowing from the vendor's audience as well.

Here is a list for reference. Feel free to make any of these videos or use them to get ideas for additional videos.

Videos about your city or town

- Best Investment Areas in Town
- Pros and Cons of Living in That Area
- Common Architecture
- What I Love About the Area
- Neighborhoods
- Top 3 Parks in the Area
- The 5 Best Local Restaurants
- Lowest Priced Zip Codes
- Interview Business Owners
- Highest Priced Zip Codes

Real Estate Terminology

- What is a residential purchase agreement?
- What is the escrow process?
- What is a good earnest deposit?
- What is title insurance
- What is a Federal Housing Administration (FHA) home loan?
- What is a home inspection?
- What is equity?
- What is private mortgage insurance (PMI)?
- What is a homeowner association (HOA)?
- What is _____?

Videos for Buyers

- What is a Buyer's Agent?
- Do I Need 20% Down to Buy a Home?
- How Much Can You Afford?
- How to Find the Perfect Home?
- 3 Things You Can Do to Prepare to Buy Your First Home
- 3 Tips to Improve Your Credit Score
- What Documents Will I Need for a Pre-Approval?
- How to Negotiate Repairs While Buying a Home
- The Difference Between Rent and Mortgage
- How Many Homes Should You See Before You Make an Offer?
- Who Pays the Realtor's Commission?
- 3 Tips for Buying New Construction
- Avoid These 3 Buyers Mistakes and Save Money
- Do You Need to Get a Home Inspection?
- Interview with a Past Client
- Offer Accepted! Now What?
- How Much Money Do I Need to Buy a Home?
- What's the Difference Between a Condo, Townhouse, or Single-Family Home?

Videos for Sellers

- 3 Ways to Get More Money When You Sell
- Do You Need to Stage Your Home?
- Pre-List Maintenance Checklist
- How to Price Your Home to Sell
- In What Season Should You Sell Your Home?
- The Home Selling Process
- The Home Selling Timeline
- Who Pays the Listing Agents Commission?

SOCIAL MEDIA

- Why Curb Appeal Matters!
- 3 Low-Cost Improvements to Make Before You List
- What Happens if Your Home Doesn't Appraise?
- Current Market Update
- 3 Interior Colors Getting the Most Attention

No excuses! These are all videos anyone of you can make. Start with the one you know the best and fully understand. If you don't understand the question yourself or any part of it, do your research. When one teaches, two learn. Create a list of videos and keep it handy. I have a running list in the notes section of my phone.

PRO TIP: *Anytime you hear a good topic or issue, pull out your phone and put it in your notes. I do this all the time. If you do this, too, you will never run out of topics because you'll train your brain to look for opportunities every day.*

3 ACTION STEPS

1. Choose what platforms on which to focus.
2. Create your brand using the worksheets on this book.
3. Create your posting schedule for each week, each month, and for the year.

"I love open houses because there's no rejection involved. Potential buyers are coming to see what I have to sell."

— JEFF DISCHER

CHAPTER 7

OPEN HOUSES

Let Clients Come to You

Have you ever gone car shopping right after you purchased your car, or how about when you weren't in the market at all? Didn't think so. Neither do people looking to buy or sell a home. Open houses are a way to bring people to you that are either: in the market to buy, in the market to sell, or will be one of the two in the near future. It's very hard to get rejected while holding open houses. These people are coming to you to find out information about the product you have to sell. Information can be the price, size, bed- and bath count, why the owner is selling, the seller's motivation, if you can help them write the offer, identify the comps, etcetera. What this means is you have the opportunity to shine. Don't do what most agents do, which is to show up five minutes before the open house, set up with a few signs, and stare at their watch until it's over so they can go do the other things they want to do. Who wants to work with someone like that? I don't. I want someone who treats me well and who takes their career seriously and is professional.

There are a couple of ways to shine while holding open houses. **Presentation** and **Market Knowledge.** Both are equally important and deserve to be mastered. Clients will notice the difference between your open house and the other ten they attended that day. That's the goal. Stand out in as many ways as possible while staying composed and professional.

The **Open House Presentation** needs to be aggressive in a professional, appealing way. It needs to speak your brand whether that brand is you, your team, or your company. You need to take ownership and pride in each open house you do and imagine doing it to sell a very important home or investment. Act as if you are doing every open house for your parents' home so they can retire. The point is to take pride in your open houses when considering presentation so you can command the most competitive offers.

Pay attention to the details. If you've been to open houses before, then you know there are good ones, and there are bad ones. There are the open houses run by professionals, and then there are the half-ass open houses run out of desperation. I've done both. I get it. Once you start treating each open house like a professional, you will see the difference immediately. The goal is to stand out from the other open houses that the potential buyer has seen that weekend and to get them to remember yours more favorably than the others.

> **PRO TIP:** *Drive around this weekend and look at open houses in your neighborhood. Notice the signage count and placement. Are there flags on the signs? Are the signs strategically placed for maximum visibility? Are the signs easy to read and understandable? Go into the open house and notice how the real estate agent greets you.*

Are they in your face or passive? Which do you like better as a guest? Which makes you feel better? How has the real estate agent presented themselves? Well put together and prepared? They should be. Take mental notes for yourself and your future open houses. Notice the real estate agents' setup. Is it clean and organized? Does it feel inviting? How does the home smell?

The key is to put yourself in the buyer's shoes and understand how they would feel walking into that open house. When you're done with five to ten open houses, write a list of what you liked and didn't like about the open houses—the pro and cons. Now take the pros and use that as a foundation for your open houses. You want your open houses to better than any other open house you attended.

Now, ALL open houses are NOT the same nor equal. As I said before, the average agent shows up five minutes before their open house, throws a few signs out, prints out a couple of multiple listing service (MLS) flyers, and stares at their watch for three hours thinking of what they are going to do after the open house. What a waste of time. They are wasting their time, and they're wasting the seller's time. The professional maximizes the open house by creating an experience, knowing that the perfect buyer could be walking through the door at any minute. Then there's the chance a neighbor could walk in and mention she wants to sell her home down the street as well. You will stand out and increase the chances of at least getting your foot in the door for an interview by being prepared and delivering valuable information while at the same having the best open house setup in the neighborhood. Every person who walks through that door is a possible new client relationship. They may be a client today, or they may be a client in eighteen months—regardless, it's a new client who needs your help but only if you can show you care and that you have a decent amount of knowledge. Be real with people. If, based on your conversations, you know there is a house down the street that would be a better fit, tell them about it. Being real and transparent sells. Patience sells. This is critical because I've seen clients drop their agents right there at the open house, and they do so because of the experience the agent created at the open house that day. They do so because the agent didn't care, didn't demonstrate a decent amount of knowledge, wasn't real, didn't listen, or wasn't transparent. It's real. There's a difference.

DO NOT HAVE COMMISSION BREATH!

What's that? That is when you come across as desperate and pushy to your clients because you're broke and need the money. They feel your desperation. **VERY BAD MOVE!**

> **PRO TIP:** *We've all heard of* **ABC—Always Be Closing!** *Let me ask you a question. Do you like to be closed? Have you ever purchased something and called a friend and said, "I got closed today!"? I don't think so. So why try to "close" someone? That term makes me feel like I'm making someone do something they don't want to do. That doesn't feel good. Karma is real. I prefer* **NBC— Never Be Closing!** *I prefer asking as many questions as possible to determine if it's even a good deal for the client. Do they need it based on everything you've heard so far? Do you need to continue asking more questions? Questions are the answer. The goal is to provide value, listen, educate when needed, and let the person make an honest decision. If you do your job correctly, they will buy if they need it and not if they don't.*

OPEN HOUSES

Open houses are the perfect place to meet new clients and start to build your database. Host your open house the Discher Group way, and you will make a professional and lasting impression. (For the list of items you need to you consistently stand out at your open houses, see Appendix I: Host a Six-Figure Open House.)

> **PRO TIP:** *Use a professional registration app on an e-tablet to have visitors sign in and capture info. (Use a write-in sheet if you don't have a tablet.)*
>
> **PRO TIP:** *Have a roll-out banner branded with your picture on it with credentials, team, and/or company. It's about $150 and well worth it. Your local sign printing and promotion firm can whip it up in a few days.]*
>
> **PRO TIP:** *Tour the property the day before and film a short video. Edit it with your film editing app and use that to promote along with still photos you get from the Internet.*

Looking the part and standing out is to get potential buyers to stop the car and come into the property. The other part of the equation is having the **Market Knowledge** or at least the ability to have it at your fingertips so you can build competent trust. People want to hire a person who is competent. The good news about the ease of information is that we can get the stats and comparable properties for an area in minutes, if not seconds from our phone or laptops, with the right knowledge and know-how. What does this mean? It means that you don't need to be a neighborhood "expert" anymore to be the best at the job. Nancy, who's been farming that area for thirty-four years, may have a "coming soon" that I don't know about, but that's about it. You have to know and understand your phone, tablet, laptop, and the Internet. We have all the information and technology at our fingertips. You can pull all the information the night before or the day of and have your data ready and accessible to answer any questions someone may have that you don't know. You need to have a basic understanding of the home and its surroundings. The more you know, the better. Do your research beforehand and only rely on your phone the day of for additional information to support you.

- **Rule:** *Start by looking for open houses available in the area you know best. That's the easiest way to start. If you can't find anything available in that community, try the one you know next best and so on. Regardless of where your open house is located, do your due diligence and know what you're selling.*

It's very easy to prepare and do even better with the current technology out there today. Here is some information to have available:

- The most recently sold comparable properties in the area.
- The comparable active homes in the area. They may want something the subject property doesn't have, and you can show them after you're done with your open house. You can email them a list of other available properties in the area: boom, new client.
- A list of any upgrades the subject property may have.
- The schools in the area and the school districts.
- The highlights of the area: parks, schools, easy access to freeways, shopping, dining.

The sharper and more dialed-in your open house, the more memorable. Answer questions. Become their resource and authority as fast as possible. The more memorable, the more likely they are to call you when they have a question. Be the one they think to call when it's time to buy or sell a home. That's the goal. Be sharp. Be intentional. Sell that house.

NEVER BE PUSHY!

How many open houses should you hold a week? Here's the open house power schedule for those agents who are genuinely committed to six figures. Lazy agents will say it's too much, and they're right. If you are going for average, stick with the basics. If you want to break through the six-figure ceiling and establish a solid database, do it this way.

Host at least five to seven open houses if you have zero homes in escrow.

Please remember two things: 1) it doesn't have to be your listing to host the open house, and 2) open houses are only two or three hours each. Even at seven days a week, that's a max of twenty-one hours in any given week. That's about a third of your week doing open houses. Not bad for the amount of freedom that will eventually come. Put in the hard work now, and the success will accompany by default. Starting your real estate business is like getting a plane off the ground; it takes everything it has, full throttle to get the plane off the ground, and once you're up to cruising altitude you can pull back on the throttle.

You need to work very hard and very long hours in the beginning until you start to build momentum with your database and get those first few deals. Actually, it will take until after your first thirty or forty deals to get a decent understanding of the business and what is needed just to survive and what is required in order to thrive!

If you're going to do it, go all the way. Create the life you always desired! Do the DAMN open houses, and don't complain. Even if you complain, still do them. Learn to love doing them and learn to love the open house process because this is a sure way to build your database. You want to use your open houses and social media to meet and develop relationships with people. Eventually, they end up in your database and one day will be your clients. And the people they know become clients as well.

This is the schedule to which I hold my agents accountable:

If you have ...	Then you need to conduct ...
0 homes in escrow	5 to 7 open houses per week
1 home in escrow	4 to 5 open houses per week
2 homes in escrow	3 to 4 open houses per week
3 homes in escrow	2 to 3 open houses per week
4 homes in escrow	1 to 2 open houses per week

PRO TIP: *Do the same open house until it sells. The neighbors will see your name every day coming and going and may stop and ask about selling their home. Additionally, you don't have to waste more time finding another available open house.*

PRO TIP: *Prioritize hosting open houses that are near busy intersections. They tend to get more traffic. Unless it's your own listing, then always do the one you listed first.*

3 FOUNDATIONAL STEPS TO A SUCCESSFUL OPEN HOUSE

1. Go out this weekend and look at open houses. Take notes of the pros and cons you observe. Use this information to create your open house experience. This part of the process will save you valuable time and money.

OPEN HOUSES

> 2. Search and seek out available open houses in your area. Reach out to the listing agents and ask if you can hold open houses for their listings.
> 3. Hold five to seven open houses per week; use a custom branded template for flyers; and set up open house signs the morning of the open house, not five minutes before.

Reach out to listing agents, requesting permission to hold open houses for one or more of their listings, and it's a win-win for everyone. (For a template to use in reaching out to listing agents via email or text message, see Appendix I: Host a Six-Figure Open House.) You get open house opportunities, positioning you to get in front of others to hone your skills as an agent, and the listing agents get to tell sellers that their homes will be held open daily. You're probably asking, "Jeff, why wouldn't the listing agent not just hold it open?" Great question. Some will, but most will not because they have other listings or because they are too lazy or too busy. You are doing them a favor by holding open one or more of their listings. ALWAYS approach it with that mindset. Don't be scared. You are helping them just as much they are helping you.

I have listed many homes—hundreds even—and I can tell you from experience, when I get a listing and get calls from other agents wanting to hold it open, there are things I look for before I agree. It can be a win-win or a lose-lose. If you let the wrong person hold open your listing, it could be all bad. I once let an agent hold open one of my listings, and she showed up an hour late and drunk. People were calling me from my "for sale" sign, letting me know a drunk lady in my listing claimed to be a real estate agent and was holding an open house. They told me "She wouldn't give us the keys or let us past the front door. She smelled like alcohol." No bueno.

But it can also work out well. The final point is to stand out! Become a master at holding open houses. It will not only support and feed your buyer pool, but it will help you get more listings. People notice good work. By having an amazing open house and documenting it through social media, people can see what you're doing and compare it to other realtors' efforts. If the open house and video are done well, then you may get the job as the listing agent or buyer's agent from one of your viewers! Well, that's the goal.

> ### 3 ACTION STEPS
> 1. Design and order open house signs.
> 2. Map out the neighborhood you want to hold an open house. Search for vacant homes on the market in that area to find your possible open houses.
> 3. Schedule the one that is newest on the market and closest to busy intersections.

CHAPTER 8

DATABASE

Stay in Front of the People Who Know You

What is your **database**? Your database is comprised of people who know you, typically like and trust you, and may or may not have used your real estate services before. You have all their information stored in a customer relationship manager (CRM) or a contact database of some sort like Google Contacts, Yahoo, smartphone, or an excel spreadsheet, and you have the ability to contact them on a regular basis. There's a saying, "A bird in the hand is better than two in a bush." You **MUST** take care of the contacts in your database first. I'll repeat, these people know who you are; treat them well and stay in the forefront of their mind.

For the most part, the hard part is done. You have an organized database. Your job is to mind them and build that list. Set goals to add people to your database and make sure your follow-up is

"It takes months to find a customer… seconds to lose one."

– VINCE LOMBARDI

efficient and maximized with all the different communication platforms and tools available. Each contact should be touched at least once every one to three months with a personal message depending on the relationship. When I say depending on the relationship, are they currently looking for homes with you, or is there a home currently on the market for sale, or are they past clients? Active clients are getting talked to much more than your past clients or clients who are eighteen months out from buying or selling a home. Yes, eighteen *months*—not a typo—out. Some of your clients will be two years out. These contacts going along at a slower pace make up what is called your **sales pipeline**. In the sense that I'm using it, your sales pipeline could be thought of as a linear timeline starting today and extending out two years with all your potential clients and when they would be buying or selling a home.

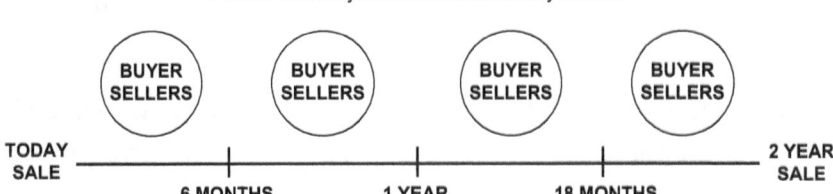

Each group of buyers and sellers above will be ready for business someday. And I'll tell you this, in real estate, time flies. There have been times my clients have called me up to sell their home, and I'm thinking, you just bought that home. I look at my CRM and discover it was four years ago when they purchased and closed. Time flies. I am in front of current, past, and future clients multiple times per year, every year from the moment I meet them, and years still fly by like minutes, it seems. You will wake up one day, and your eighteen-month-later buyers and sellers will be calling you up to facilitate their transaction.

You must keep your pipeline as full as possible at all times. That's why we NEVER discount the prospects that say they are eighteen to twenty-four months away from making a move. I'm not joking when I say this, most agents hear eighteen to twenty-four months out of the mouth of potential clients, and they are on to the next one. That's too long for them. They're shortsighted. They want RIGHT NOW business. I'll tell you, if you ignore the people you already know, you won't have any business RIGHT NOW.

When you are intentionally staying in front of your current and potential clients, you should be leveraging all platforms for communication, including social media (don't forget direct messaging), postcards, emails, texts, video messages, pop-by's, and phone calls to stay in front of your clients in the right ways. Always giving excellent value without being annoying. Be authentic and check-in. Your clients want to hear from you as long as you're not trying to shove real estate and sales down their throats. There's a WAY!

> **PRO TIP:** *Are you scared to call your database? Most agents are because they don't know what to say. There's an easy acronym to use:* **F.O.R.D.**
>
> *Ask the person you are calling about their ...*
>
>   *Family (spouse, significant other, children)*
>
>   *Occupation (career/job/business)*
>
>   *Recreation (what they've been doing lately such as travel, hobbies, sports)*
>
>   *Dreams (whether they're working on anything new or have any big plans for the future)*

> **PRO TIP:** *In your CRM database, note the names of your client's family members and keep track of life transitions. Contact them immediately for birthdays, weddings, graduations, and other special moments in their lives, but don't be afraid to reach out when you learn of a death, a divorce, or another sad occasion in the family. You want to reach out with authenticity and care about what is going on in their life.*

I am not a big fan of scripts. I'm not saying don't use them; I'm just saying I've never really depended on them. There's been a few I thought were helpful that I've manipulated and made my own by internalizing them. I suggest you do the same so that you have context and responses to keep the relationship moving forward when first working with a new client. I give my agents script books and have them read them before they start calling, and that's it. Once you start calling, put the scripts away and come from the heart. People feel when you're scripted, and they feel when you care. I believe in understanding people. Ask a shit-ton of questions and listen very carefully. Have an insightful, discovering conversation with your client. Do what's right for your client at all times. **THAT'S THE SCRIPT.** Using scripts seems like a form of closing, and you know how I feel about that. They are not all bad, though. Some help people feel comfortable picking up the phone.

Using the **F.O.R.D.** acronym should make it a lot easier to have a conversation. You probably already feel more confident calling your prospects. As you're contacting your database, make sure you have your CRM open to that person's profile so you can document what they tell you when you're asking them the questions. This is very important, and you will need this information. Example: You call your past client Mike to check-in. You say hello and start running through the F.O.R.D. system. When you ask about family, Mike tells you about his son Joey that just started soccer last week, and he loves it, his wife received a promotion at work, and his parents just retired. Great information and you have documented it all in your CRM. A few months later, when it's time for another call, it goes something like this:

You: *"Hey Mike. It's me, Jeff Discher, your favorite REALTOR®.* (Yes, I say this. They always laugh, and it breaks the ice. Another great line is, "Hey, Mike. I'm calling with my REALTOR® hat on today.") *I'm calling to check in per usual. How's everything going?"*
Mike: *"Great!"*
You: *"How's little Joey's soccer coming along?"*
Mike: *"Really Good. They actually put him as goalie because he was so aggressive."*
You: *"How's your wife liking her new job?"*
Mike: *"She loves it. They let her work from home twice a week, which is nice."*
You: *"And I'm sure your parents have already been on a few vacations."*

You see what is happening here. I'm continuing where we left off from our last conversation. It shows I was listening and cared. The client will be impressed. They always are. These are the little things that make the difference. These are the small details, but they are things that get you referrals. These are the things that bring you making six figures in your next twelve months as a real estate agent.

> **PRO TIP:** *Smile when you answer and speak on the phone. The person on the other side can hear it.*

DATABASE

Let's start with organizing your database. If you are starting from scratch, so much the better! Get together all databases you currently have, including personal phone contacts, google contacts, Yahoo contacts, all other email contacts, old phone books you may have names and numbers written in, social media friends, co-workers from previous jobs, and any other place names and numbers may be. These are all the people that made their way into your personal database at some point or another. You may have some people in one place and some in another. You may have friends on social media, but you don't have their phone numbers, emails, or addresses. Collect these bits of information from everyone. Don't be shy. Reach out via direct messenger (DM) and ask. If you're good enough friends, they shouldn't have a problem with it. If you don't feel comfortable asking them, you need to build a stronger relationship through time and communication.

When people initially do this, they typically have a very high number of contacts. They have complied four hundred to six hundred names. Remember, I'm talking about ALL contacts. At first glance, it looks like a great database to start with until it is dissected. What do I mean by dissected? The average person will lose between half to three-quarters of their database once they remove all the people from that list that you know would never buy, sell, send you a referral, or just don't know or remember. It's okay, though; you now have an actual list. The list may shrink again slightly when you start reaching out to these people. Wrong or bad numbers, moved out of state or country, or tell you never to call again. Again, it's okay. The goal from that moment on is to make it a weekly plan to add three or more people to your database.

What qualifies someone to add to your database? You either meet them in person face-to-face, by phone, email, or some form of formal introduction with the intent to someday help them buy or sell real estate. Business cards help this goal. Always carry five business cards in your pocket and make it a goal to hand them all out by the end of each day. Some will turn into real conversations, and you can exchange information and add them to your database, or at a minimum, you hand out a card to a stranger that may someday call you. This exercise is arduous but worth its weight in gold. Some of the highest-paid people I know hand their cards to everyone they come in contact. It's something I still work on today. My role is different now, although it's still a goal.

Go through all your contacts and put next to each one a **1, 2, 3, or 4**. Please remember the intent of this exercise is that you are building a database of people for your real estate business:

1. **Advanced Fans** | These people hold you in high regard when it comes to your profession. Also known as "Raving Fans" (the moniker given by the same-titled book by Ken Blanchard and Sheldon Bowles), these can be past clients or people who have watched you and know how well you do your job. We've all had one or two, maybe three people who we go to for a particular service. They stand out. That person could be a mechanic, a car detailer, an insurance agent, a plumber, an electrician, a tire place, a maid or housekeeper, a personal trainer, a chef, an attorney, or any other profession. When you think of that industry, you automatically think of that person. You may even recommend them before to someone who asks. These people will typically send you between two to three referrals a year.

    Action Plan | These people receive your monthly newsletter and meet with you once a month face-to-face over coffee or a meal at your expense. The goal is to get ten of these people in your database. Hard, yet doable. Imagine having ten people you like and who like you, basically friends, sending you business all year. With an average of thirty deals done by referral, that's a pretty good year.

2. **Fans** | These people know you and like you, and they may even talk to people they know about how good you are as a realtor. These people typically send you one deal a year. Much better than most. These people are still very important and should be handled with care as well. Someday these amazing people may be become Advanced Fans.

   Action Plan | These people receive the monthly newsletter as well as a personal contact every two months.

3. **Friendly Acquaintances** | These people know you and like you but haven't sent you business yet. It could be for several reasons. First, they just don't hang out with anyone that is buying or selling homes. Second, they are afraid to refer anyone because they are scared it may go south. Third, they have a family member or closer friend that they refer. The list goes on. The good news is this group could always move up the ladder—if treated correctly—to become a fan or advanced fan. Treat them correctly!

   Action Plan | These people receive the monthly newsletter and a call once a quarter (once every three months). So, check-in to see how they're doing, and don't forget about them. All it takes is being in the right place at the right time for these people to drop your name, and BOOM, they are a fan.

4. **Who are these people?** | These are basically just names. These could be people you met on the fly, old girlfriends or boyfriends that you don't talk to at all anymore, people you wouldn't want to work with even if they wanted to, and anyone you know who

will never buy a home or refer anyone to you. Not bad or good; you just know they will not send you business.

Action Plan | You can send them a newsletter if you wish; however, these are not the people you want to prioritize.

The goal is to build a robust database from the start. It will save you time and efficiency in the long run. When you are first starting, most names will be in the bottom two categories. So again, go through everything you have and put a number next to them. The goal is to get them classified and into your CRM. This will be the beginning of your real estate database.

Once you get down to your actual number and all entered into your CRM, you can organize them again. You can call the groups of clients whatever you want at that point because you will know your plan for each level of contacts.

Here's how I organize my contacts:

- **Current Buyers** | These are buyers that pre-approved with a lender and actively looking for homes to buy.
- **Buyers 6–12 Months Out** | These are buyers that have to wait or will be ready to purchase a home within the next 6–12 months. They may be getting a new job, moving to the area, repairing their credit, getting an inheritance for a down payment, etc.
- **Current Sellers** | There are homes that are on the market or in escrow.
- **Sellers 6–12 Months Out** | These are sellers that need to sell within 6–12 months. The home may need remodeling, making repairs, waiting for a particular value before they sell, or the person could be waiting for a job transfer.
- **Past Clients** | These are people you have already helped buy or sell a home.

- **Friends and Family** | Self-explanatory. These may be in multiple sections, and your CRM may allow you to add multiple tags or categories. You typically see these people more often than clients.
- **Professional Colleagues** | This would be my vendor team that consists of other agents with whom I've done business to included, but not limited to, plumbers, electricians, inspectors, lenders, etcetera.
- **Inactive leads** | These are people who haven't purchased from you but may someday.
- **Business Networking International (BNI)** | This is a business networking group of which I am a member.

Now your database is organized. Make sure each person's profile is filled out as much as possible and includes their birthdays, home purchase anniversaries, wedding anniversaries, children's names and birthdays, email, address, pet names, work addresses, social media pages, and any notes that you can refer to in the future. You can go into your CRM and set alerts and programs for all the special dates. You will get reminded, and you just fulfill the task. Call. Text. Email. Notecard. BOOM.

3 ACTION STEPS

1. Collect all your contacts from all your current and past databases.
2. Organize them in a range of 1 to 4 between "Advanced Fans" and "Who Are These People?"
3. Organize the final list and input it into your CRM by the classifications you've chosen.

SUMMARY

There is a lot to do to establish your business on a solid foundation—the good news is that the work is hard but simple. Real estate is a very simple business; it's just not easy.

When I started my real estate career in 2004, the company I worked for had exhaustive and intensive training for new agents covering dozens of tactics to get your first transaction under your belt. This was back before technology made it easier to batch and streamline some lead generation tactics. At Discher Group, I help my agents focus on three main strategies to jumpstart their first six figures:

Social Media – view every interaction on social media platforms as you walking into a networking event. Use your phone to post thoughtfully created videos that provide value about the industry to potential clients. Better yet, pay attention to the videos you like to watch on Facebook or YouTube to be aware of why you like them. Next time you come across a video you like, take note as to why you like it.

Open Houses – let clients come to you by hosting open houses. When you start, you may be hosting for listings other than your own, and that is alright. Do market research on the area and have a professional presentation to wow the people who attend. Stand out in as many ways as possible while staying composed and professional. Dress well, and brand everything. BOOM. I mean everything from your signs leading into the open house to your laptop and phone case, every piece of marketing should be designed to make a lasting impression. Remember to make sure that you do not have commission breath! Do not come from a place of scarcity or desperation. Instead focus on providing value to each person who attends the open house.

DATABASE

Database – set goals to add people to your database and make sure your follow-up is efficient and maximized with all the different communication platforms and tools available. Each contact should be touched at least once every one to three months with a personal message depending on the relationship. NEVER discount the prospects who say they are eighteen to twenty-four months away from making a move.

Start building your database from Day 1 and categorize the people in your network with a 1, 2, 3, or 4 based on how they figure into your real estate business:

1 – **Advanced Fans** are people may be past clients or people who have watched you and know how well you do your job. They will typically send you two to three referrals a year. Your goal is to get ten of these "raving fans" in your database. Meet these people once a month face-to-face over coffee or a meal at your expense.

2 – **Fans** are people you know and who like you. They typically send you one deal a year. Handle these people with care since they may someday become Advanced Fans. Send them a monthly newsletter and initiate personal contact every two months.

3 – **Friendly Acquaintances** are people who know you and like you but who haven't sent you business yet. These people receive the monthly newsletter and a call once a quarter (every three months). Check-in to see how they're doing, and don't forget about them. All it takes is being in the right place at the right time for these people to drop your name, and BOOM, they are a fan.

4 – **Who are These People?** are just names—people with whom you wouldn't want to work even if they wanted to work with you. They aren't bad or good; you just know they will not send

you business. You can send them a newsletter if you wish; however, these are not the people you want to prioritize.

Use your CRM to gather vital information like birthdays, anniversaries, and the names of people important to their family, such as a spouse, children, and pets.

Your real estate business will be ready to scale if you master your social media, open houses and database. Now you are ready to learn how to invest in your business.

INVEST IN YOUR BUSINESS

"It is essential to have good tools, but it is also essential that the tools should be used in the right way."

– WALLACE D. WATTLES

CHAPTER 9

SUCCESS TOOLS

What it Takes to Run Your Business Successfully

Building a real estate business will require tools of some sort. Consider any job or career, and when you really think about it, there are some necessary tools needed. If you're a chef, you have knives, pots, pans, utensils, aprons, ovens, stoves, refrigerators, spices, produce, proteins—all the accoutrements necessary to perform as a chef. If you are a doctor, then you have your scrubs, lights, operating room, and operating tools, such as scalpels, gloves, masks, stethoscopes, and so on. My point is that with every job, you can think of requires specialized tools, supplies, or uniforms required to perform. The same goes for real estate. If you want a successful and extraordinary career, you must set up your office and environment to win. If you were starting your career as a chef, as mentioned above, how successful do you think you would be if you had none of the tools needed to prepare and cook food? Even if you had all the ingredients but no knives, spatula, pots, pans, utensils, and a stove, all you would have is ingredients. You may be able to make a couple of dishes; however, your dishes would be limited, and your career probably wouldn't last very long. Now I'm not saying you must have **ALL** the tools to win and become successful; I'm saying the faster you can implement everything needed, the faster the process will be. You can start with ambition, motivation, and the will to become a superstar. However, you will eventually need some tools especially if you want to operate and reach top levels in any field.

In this chapter, we will discuss some of the tools you will need to not only start your real estate career but to scale and make six figures in your next twelve months as a real estate agent. I'm not saying this is the be-all-end-all list you need either. You may find that you don't need or use some, and you may also find a bunch more that you find extremely useful that you can add to your toolbox. The list I am providing is what my team is currently implementing and utilizing to a measure of defined success. As you know, technology becomes obsolete overnight, so by the time you read this, there may be a better option available. Business concepts will hopefully remain the same but with better technology. The right tools can accelerate and organize your business, making it a lot more efficient and with less stress. It's better to start with as much in place as possible than to wait until it's needed.

When you start to scale, you must be organized and efficient. I've learned the hard way playing it by ear, and it has caused me excessive amounts of unneeded stress. It also held me back from reaching maximum achievement for years. I'm still learning and evolving my business and constantly searching for the newest tools, technology, and apps to run my business more efficiently, to communicate better, to produce the best marketing materials, to stay in front of clients better, and to stay organized better. I am always looking to be progressive, and you should too. Stay ahead of the curve. Always have your eyes and ears open for the newest trends in the business. That's what makes a great agent. Please remember, you don't need every tool available. Just because a tool or process works for someone else doesn't mean it will or has to work for you. Speak with other agents and brokers and discuss what they are utilizing and why. How is it working for them? Most experienced agents will tell you all about their trials and tribulations. Pay attention, listen, and learn. Use the Internet to check reviews as well. You will start using some tools, then realize they don't fit into your business model, or you find yourself just not using the tools efficiently and effectively; but there are some basics that everyone must have.

What tools would someone need to run a successful real estate business? When I say tools, I mean anything that will help you stay motivated, organized, efficient, stand out from the competition, and most importantly, provide the best customer service to your client. When you're first starting, I understand that forking out cash for real estate tools may not be a top priority, or you may not have the resources. The sooner you can get a solid system in place, the sooner you can scale, sell more homes in less time while having more time for yourself. That's the goal, right? I hope so, for your sake and your team's. Do what you can and put in place what you can with what you have at the moment. As you start to close deals and re-invest back into your business, you can start accumulating and building the correct infrastructure. Never question putting money back into your business. Some tools will make you substantial amounts of money, and some will cost you. Either way, it's a learning experience. Take note and move on in the way that makes the most sense for your business goals.

We could even take it a step further and say that the ultimate goal is to run a super successful real estate business (whatever that means to you) while not feeling like you're working. Can this be accomplished? Does it sound crazy to live a life of work that feels like you're doing what you love and not working a day in your life? It may now, but not for long. The life we spoke about at the beginning of the book is possible for you.

Imagine your real estate business is a home that you are building. I want to cover the tools you will need to build this house. I suggest implementing as much of it as you will use. You know how you work. Some of the tools are very basic, and some may require some practice. It gets addicting in a good way. I think.

REAL ESTATE TOOLS

Real Estate license – This one seems pretty self-explanatory, although I still must mention it. Yes, this book is based on you currently being licensed, in the process of getting licensed, or having concrete plans of getting your real estate license in the near future. If you don't have your license yet, not a big deal; you can get your license for about $500 and three months of time. That's the easy part. There are a variety of real estate schools, both online and in-person, that you can attend. If you search for real estate schools on the Internet, you will find many options from which to choose.

> **PRO TIP:** *A strategy I recommend for newer agents who aren't yet licensed is to take the three mandatory classes needed to get your test date for the final exam through the state, then sign up for a* **two-day real estate exam crash course.** *Do not study. I repeat, do not study.*

Yes, I sound crazy. When you take a test, you study, right? I would typically agree. However, in my almost twenty years of selling homes and helping people get licensed, I have found this tip to be the best *advice I could give. I've had agents not listen and fail multiple times until they finally decided to listen to my unconventional advice, and they passed. Please don't think I'm saying this is the only way; I just know it works very well.*

Your test will be on a weekday. Sign up for the two-day crash course for the weekend before your test. Do not study. Wake up the day of the crash course after getting a good night's sleep, drink a glass of water; eat a light breakfast, if any; drink a large cup of coffee; and get to class. The instructor will teach you how to pass the test, not how to sell real estate. The real work and learning start once you actually begin working for a broker. Good luck. If you're already licensed, let's move on!

Smartphone – Your smartphone is your lifeline to the world. It's your direct line to your clients, the Internet, your calendar, your database, your camera, the applications you will use every day to build your business, your photos, multiple listing service (MLS) to search for properties and get details, open lockboxes, use your customer relationship manager (CRM) (more on that tool in a moment), provides a map and directions, makes property videos, makes educational videos, timer and alarm, measuring application for room size, and much more. You can literally run your entire real estate business and life from your phone. This makes everything very convenient and efficient.

As you know by now, I'm a huge fan of efficiency. The more efficient you are in your day-to-day, the more time you have for other projects, travel, family, or whatever your little heart desires. Twenty years ago, you would need a briefcase; today, it's all in your pocket. I have used the iPhone for my entire career. I am used to it, and I feel it has all the apps I need, in addition to an awesome camera. It only seems to get better and do more. Do your research and find one you not only like, but more importantly, will use. My entire team uses the iPhone. It syncs easily with everything else as well. Plus, it's sexy and fits our style.

> **PRO TIP:** *Buy a gimbal or stabilizer for your iPhone or camera. It will make your videos smooth, cinematic, and professional. You will thank me for this $150 investment. Ronin, DJI, and EVO are good brands.*

Laptop/Tablet – Although most tasks can be handled by your phone, you will also need a laptop, a tablet, or both. When it comes to writing offers, contracts, and other documents, the laptop makes it much easier and convenient although you can just add a keyboard to your tablet. In my experience, the phone just isn't efficient or large enough to draw up a contract or read one in its entirety. The good news is once you write up the paperwork, you can still sign on your mobile device. Hopefully, sometime in the near future, we will be able to easily use all the programs on our phones in a way that makes it convenient. The tablet helps when it comes to marketing and editing as well. Creating on a larger screen is convenient for the fingers and easier on the eyes. The video editing apps can get very detailed when you're adding several layers of effects and pop-ups. I edited videos on my phone up until recently when I switched to a 12.9-inch iPad Pro. It was a game-changer. It's making editing fun again, and I can get back to making entertaining videos the way I like.

Customer Relationship Manager (CRM) – CRM software acts as your single source for all your client information and communication. Some can even hold all your client documents from start to finish and serve as a vault for long-term storage of executed contracts and home inspections. This tool is essential for running an efficient pipeline without letting clients and leads slip through the cracks. Unfortunately, some of the newer agents can't afford a CRM initially and have horror stories of losing deals and clients because they failed to follow up because they had no system in place.

One of the hardest parts of real estate is getting and converting leads and referrals. The way you get leads and referrals is by being a great agent, providing top-notch service, having excellent communications skills, and staying in front of your clients. A CRM is a perfectly designed tool to do so and do it well. It organizes all your contacts into a database and lets you run your business on a single platform. It also allows you to create different groups of clients, past clients, vendors, friends, family, buyers, sellers, and so on, making it easy to keep track of your communication and any events happening in your clients' lives. You can also set up birthday reminders, track anniversaries of home sales, manage your pipeline, automate your tasks and workflow, keep track of all your communications, and know exactly what you said and talked about the last time you spoke with each client. It alerts you every morning and gives you daily tasks to ensure you are consistent and efficient with client database follow-up. Essentially, a CRM allows salespeople to spend more time with clients and marketing, which leads to more deals closed and a stronger client base. Again, there are a bunch of different systems out there. Do your research and find the one you will use. Most of them will give you a thirty-day trial. I would sign up and dabble. Play with them and see which one seems the easiest for you to use. Write down what you think you will need it for most and make that task a priority when researching.

I personally use Contactually and have done so since 2012—back when it was a standalone product. Compass owns them now, and it is still great. I chose this one because it not only works well and is easy to use, but it's also compatible with my laptop and smartphone. When I studied what the highest-producing agents in the industry were using at the time, it was Contactually. I was at a huge Keller Williams family reunion event when I heard agents and teams doing 1,200 to 1,900 deals per year. Most were using Contactually. It has worked out well for me, and everyone I have recommended it to seems to like it. I do not get paid by Contactually for the plug; I'm just honestly impressed. Here are a few others: Top Producer, Salesforce, Juniper Square, LionDesk, Pipedrive, and Wise Agent. Again, any one of these sucks if you don't use them. If you want to save time and frustration today and in the future, I highly recommend getting a CRM on day one. Game-changer.

Multiple Listing Service (MLS) – The MLS allows brokers to see one another's listings of properties for sale with the goal of connecting homebuyers to sellers. This is the database used by real estate professionals looking for properties for their clients or posting a new property that is for sale. You must be licensed and pay the yearly membership dues and fees to be part of the MLS.

Each county has its own MLS, and once you join a brokerage, they will prompt you to join the correct association. Not only do you list your properties to sell and use it for compiling a list of properties for sale to send to your buyers, you can pull property tax records, map out showings and properties based on location on a map, find sales history, find out how much the current owners paid for it when they purchased, and much more. You can use the REALTORS® Property Resource (RPR) report, which is a great way to determine the value of a property before running the comps and looking into the details. Very useful. Many other great tools are available on the MLS, so make sure you take advantage and learn to use it as best as possible.

Phone Applications – Also known as apps for your phone. There are several apps you will need, not only to run your business but to market your business as well. We all have apps, know what we use them for, and know their purpose. The apps to run your business are no different. Each one serves a purpose, and you will use them all synergistically. Some are free, and some have small yearly or monthly fees attached. The free version is typically the basic version; the paid version is the PRO version. Always get the "PRO" version. It's a minimal investment compared to the return it will give you on your business. I don't believe any of them are more than one hundred dollars per year. DO IT!!! You'll thank me later.

REAL ESTATE APPS

Home Snap – This would be your local Multiple Listing Service app. This is a must for when you're on the go and need to pull a property for a client or get details while on the fly. There will be a time when you are out showing property, and your client sees a sign in a yard while you are looking at other homes and wants to see it or get details. You can whip out your cellphone and be the ever-ready authority.

Mortgage Calculator – There are a bunch of different ones available in the app store. I would check out a few and see which one is easiest for you to understand and use. These apps are great for giving your client a quick estimate of their payment on a property based on the selling price. Again, it's just an estimate, so make sure your clients know that and if they want exact numbers to refer to their preferred lender.

Sentrikey (Or whichever app you use to open doors of the homes you are showing to buyers) – This is the application that gets you into lockboxes to show homes. In San Diego, we have Sentrikey, though it may be different in your city or state. Check with your local real estate board or ask your broker. There is also a card version you can get; however, I prefer the app for convenience.

CRM – A Customer Relationship Manager (CRM) helps agents organize their daily schedules and prioritize tasks to ensure clients are not ignored, and all prospects are contacted on time and consistently. I previously discussed the CRM and the different companies that offer this software and app.

Measurement App – This is basically a digital tape measurer. Tape measures are easy to lose and often forgotten at home or the office. As real estate professionals, we want to be as valuable and helpful as possible. There will be plenty of times while out viewing a property that your clients will want or need the measurements of a room. They may want to see if their sofa or bed will fit, they may need measurements to get quotes for flooring, they may want to know how high the ceilings are, and many other measurements. Instead of carrying a tape measurer around with you, this app will allow you to take the measurements and save a picture of what you measure with the measurements in the photo. Pretty clever. Your buyers will love it.

Net Sheet App – Essential. This is an excellent app for when taking a listing or crunching numbers for a seller or investor. A Net Sheet App will allow you to put in the sale details, including what the sellers owe, what the new sales price is, plus all the fees and commissions. The bottom line is it's all about calculating the amount of the seller's proceeds check, and Net Sheet App helps you determine that. There are a few different ones in the app section of iPhone or Android. Try a few out and see which one has the best reviews and works for you. While most rely on their escrow officers to get them a net sheet, you can crank one out on command. I've done them at stoplights. At the mercy of escrow, no thank you. They are very busy, and the last thing I want to do is bug them for a net sheet or wait until they have time to get me one. Everything I ask you to do is for a reason and seller net sheets are a must to provide excellent service to your clients so make sure you have a quick way to get one.

All Social Media – When I say all social media apps, I mean all social media apps that you will use for your business. I would highly recommend: *Facebook, Instagram, YouTube, Anchor for your Podcast,*

SUCCESS TOOLS

LinkedIn, TikTok, Snapchat, Twitter, Clubhouse, and any others you may use, or that may hit the scene after this book was written. You can also use apps that help you organize and post at specific times, days, months on one, two, three, or all of your social media sites. Sites like *Hootsuite*. They save a lot of time. I truly believe the future of real estate and business is in Social Media.

MARKETING APPS

Over – Over is an application that can be used in many ways. From logo design, meme design, label design, lower third design, adding logos and watermarks to projects, flyers, marketing materials, property flyers, holiday posts for social media, holiday cards birthday posts on social media, birthday cards, banners, and basically anything related to marketing and overlay. This app will help you produce high-quality projects on the fly. I use this app every day for many different projects.

LumaFusion or any video editing app – The key is to find one you will use. There's iMovie, Vimeo, InShot, Splice, Video Editor, FilmakerPro, Adobe Premiere Clip, Magisto, and Quik App. Again, try these out and see which one fits your style and is easy to use. Some are more technical for more advanced editing, like LumaFusion, and some that are much simpler, like FilmakerPro. Video is the future so make sure you get started as soon as possible. Don't worry about the best quality at first. It's all about the content. The quality will get better by default by producing content every day.

Green Screen by Do Ink – Use Green Screen or any green screen/chroma key app. There are others out there; I just use this one due to its ease and convenience. If you aren't familiar with working with a green screen, what a green screen can do is position you to basically become the weatherman of real estate. It's great for filming videos and interchanging the backdrops without leaving the office. You will also need a green screen backdrop. You can either paint a wall in an office or go to Google or Amazon and buy a green cloth backdrop. The color code for the chroma key green is PMS Color Match Chroma Key 354c on the Pantone color system. Using the green screen is a great tool to separate you from the crowd. Get creative with it and have fun. This will help you stand out. It's also a feature in most video editing apps. I know LumaFusion has it in the app. Check your video app before getting this one as well.

Eraser – This is a great app for extracting an item from a photo. If you want to grab a logo and make it transparent, this is your app. I use it for flyers and presentations all the time. In addition, I extract books, furniture, logos, cars, and just about anything else I need for marketing purposes.

PixomaticPRO – This is pretty much the same as Eraser, but I use this one for extracting people. If you want to crop yourself out of a photo and use that image for marketing by creating a bio or a team photo, flyers, and other marketing collateral, then this is the app you need. Get the pro version; it's much easier to use and does all the work for you.

Picstitch – This allows you to put multiple pictures on one post. You can combine multiple images of a home into one photo to make it easier to view as a single image. Great for flyers, social media posts, digital vision boards, and much more. Also great for creating side-by-side comparisons. Again, I'm sure there are other apps out there that do this as well, but this is what I use. Look around and find one that fits you.

PERSONAL DEVELOPMENT APPS

YouTube – YouTube for personal development, you ask? Yes, I use this YouTube every single day to watch lectures, keynotes, interviews, podcasts, how-to videos, educational videos, property videos, recorded seminars, and much more. It's also a very powerful social media tool and way to connect. You should be housing all your videos on YouTube and then sharing the link from there. Plus, you will be uploading videos onto your account while building your personal library for your audience and online resume. This app can also serve as a search engine for other agents and clients.

Audible – If you haven't heard of Audible, you've probably been sleeping under a rock. This is the platform to house and read all your books. You should be doing both paperback reading and listening to books as well. You can buy books directly from the app, and they also give you credits. You should be using Audible at the gym, while driving, running, before you go to bed, or really doing anything that allows you to wear headphones. There are a few different audiobook apps out there, so feel free to use the one you already have or find one you will. Your public library may also have an audiobook app available for download that is linked to your library card.

12 Mins or Blinkist – These apps are the Cliffnotes of reading paperback books. They read all your favorite books and condense them into both audible and written versions that are easy to pop on whenever you have a few minutes to get some extra knowledge. I can get a refresher while steaming in the sauna at the gym—great little bonus sessions.

Google – We all know Google. Google is the everything you want to know search engine. Half the time an agent asks a question, it can be answered by Google. This is the #1 search engine for all your informational needs. You can book flights, get the answer to questions, do research on a property or neighborhoods, market yourself, and much more. There are others out there as well, like Bing and Yahoo.

There you go. Here is a essential list based on today's technology and what's available and convenient. What I share is what I use or have used. Some are more technical than others. It's what I've recommended to several agents that have made six-figures in their first 12 months as a real estate agent. This is what I encourage. Fast and convenient so you can be as efficient as possible. That's the key to not only putting out mass amounts of content, but also keeping your costs down because you can do so much yourself. And you can do it FAST. Learn to adapt and use as many of these tools as possible as soon as you can. Set your business up to scale from the get-go. It will save you a lot of time and frustration in the future.

3 ACTION STEPS

1. Download all the applications onto your phone from the App store you will be using.
2. Spend a weekend playing with all the apps, learning how to use them, and figuring out which ones to keep or lose.
3. Group all your apps appropriately and brand based on your pillars, these, and color scheme.

CHAPTER 10

BUILD LASTING RELATIONSHIPS

Create Clients for Life

The hardest part about real estate is generating a client. Getting a lead. A referral. Basically, waiting for a real person that trusts you enough to allow you to help them find or sell a home. The most significant investment of most people's lives. It's a stressful time, and people want to know they're hiring a professional. Someone that's competent and they can trust. I tell agents this every day until I'm blue in the face. Anyone can sell a house, but not everyone can get a client.

In San Diego alone, there are over 22,000 licensed real estate agents. There are currently 4,000 total homes on the market. That's just over five agents trying to sell each home. So, what do you do to not only get clients but retain them and get them to refer to your business? A study conducted by the National Association of

> *"Succeeding in business is all about making connections."*
>
> – SIR RICHARD BRANSON

BUILD LASTING RELATIONSHIPS

When realtors ask home sellers why they didn't use the realtor who originally helped them buy their home sell their home, the number one answer is that they couldn't remember who it was. They never heard from their realtor again after the sale. That's crazy to me. That means that the realtor only cared about that sale and not the client.

If they genuinely ran a business and cared about their clients, they would stay in touch with clients after the sale. They would check-in periodically to make sure their clients don't have any questions or problems with the home. They would check-in and become the authority in their market for their past clients. Not just for business either, but as a friend and advisor. Now some clients you'll be closer with than others, and that's ok. The goal is to stay in front of **all** your clients regardless of how close you are to them. You are still their real estate consultant and advisor, or at least you should be. Real estate is a relationship business that should last a lifetime.

The goal is to create clients for life. Treat them like family, and when they think of real estate or anyone asks, you're always at the top of their mind. I've heard it too many times, agents opening up Facebook or social media, and wham, the client you thought was yours just sold the home you helped them buy and closed on their new home with another agent. This is very common among agents. It doesn't feel good, and it can take the wind out of your sail very quickly. I've seen agents literally get up and go home. I've been that guy. That's one reason I go so hard and put so much energy into my database. You must stay in front of your clients and work to build a lifelong relationship. How do you do that? You use your CRM.

How do you stay in front of your clients? Do you call them every week? Do you stop by their house? Do you stop by their place of work? Do you mail them a postcard? Do you send them video messages? Do you email them? The answer is **ALL OF THE ABOVE.** That's your job before and after each home sale. Stay in touch. Wouldn't you want that if you purchased a home? I bought my first condo when I was 23 years old. The agent was referred by a buddy who said he was good. I remember the guy used some old-school tricks on me. I didn't realize it until after I was in the business a few years later. Like he would show me the worse condo in my price range at first and that the last would still be shitty, but it was better than the rest we had seen that day. Naturally, I would see the last one and tell to write up an offer. I bring it up because, after the sale, I never heard from the guy again. Ever. No closing gift. No, hey, how you are liking your place. No, hey, do you know who or how to get in touch with your homeowner association (HOA). Do you know how to have your utilities turned on? No. NADA.

One reason agents say they don't reach out to their clients is because they feel like they're bugging them. I know because I used to feel that way when I first started. Agents would come into my office every day with the same issue, *"I don't want to call these people because I don't know what to say. I just talked to them a month ago."* Do you feel that way? If so, why do you feel that way? Is it because you don't know what to say? It's a normal conversation. How about:

> *"Hey, John. It's your favorite REALTOR®, Jeff Discher. I wanted to reach and check-in as a good realtor should. How's the new home treating you and the family? Are you guys all settled in and enjoying it? Please let me know if there's anything I can do to help out or any questions I can answer. If you hear of anyone else looking to buy or sell a home, be sure to mention my name. I'd very much appreciate it. Oh, and let me know when the house warming party is; I'm there."*

The above script is written as a call. If this were an email or text, you would add your name and credentials to remind them what you do.

BUILD LASTING RELATIONSHIPS

I literally just made that up as I was typing. I'm sitting here at my desk in my living room overlooking the train station in San Diego, California, writing this book. I say that because I'm not suggesting anything but a regular check-in. There's no magic pill. There are scripts out there. They're basically the same as the one I gave you. It's a simple conversation check-in. Like you would call a cousin or old friend. And you would do it for a lifetime because you care. Just follow the F.O.R.D. Protocol from Chapter 8: Database—Stay in Front of the People Who Know You , and you'll be fine.

> **PRO TIP:** *The people you help buy a home will one day need to sell their home. You want the person they call to sell that house to be you.*

HOW SHOULD YOU COMMUNICATE

You should never feel bad about reaching out to your database unless you're worried about your own feelings and insecurities. The key is to put the client's needs first. It never feels bad to give something valuable. Continue to educate past clients about homeownership. Continue to educate "soon to be" homeowners about the home buying process.

You should also be using as many ways to communicate with your clients as possible. You also want to ask them how they prefer to communicate. This is very important. You don't want to send them ten notecards to find out later that they have a P.O. box and don't get mail at their home. You would ask this question at the initial consultation. Also, be aware of how your clients choose to communicate. If you call them and they don't answer and text you back, they're a texter. Text that client from now on and make a note in their file in your CRM.

If you text your client and they call you right away, they are a caller. Again, take note and add to your CRM and pick up the phone when you need to communicate with your client. This can happen with all platforms with all different clients. I have clients that only email me. Some message me on Facebook. Not joking. This tip is very important. Learn how your client wants to communicate and communicate like that.

Get their work address as well so you can send notecards to their place of employment. This is an excellent strategy because when they get a nice notecard from you just checking in and wishing them a great day, it should make them smile. If anyone is around, they will see it as well and will wonder what happened. Hopefully, that person you sent it to says, "It's a realtor I know. Check it out." It happens. And no one's expecting to get mail like that at their place of employment. It works. **DO IT.** Even if no one saw, your client still did, and you'll be at the top of their mind.

You can also check their social media accounts to see how active they are on the different platforms. Once you find out their top ways to connect and communicate, you add those platforms and addresses to your CRM. The strategy allows you to cycle through the different platforms. For example, you could start with a text message one month, the next month is a phone call, the next month is a notecard in the mail, the next month is an email, the next month is a video on their Facebook wall, the next month is a private message on Instagram, and so on. Now rinse and repeat. This strategy works because by utilizing all communication platforms, the client doesn't feel like you are blowing them up all the time. They just feel like you're everywhere. It also helps build your confidence as an agent and keeps you at the top of their mind because you reach out every month. Set this up from the beginning and use it.

BUILD LASTING RELATIONSHIPS

Platforms for communication you should cycle through when connecting with your database, as I just mentioned. Rotate through each platform each time you connect.

- **Phone Call** – Good old phone calls are great. They allow for the person listening to hear your emotion. Also great for explanations or long conversations. Just remember, unless it's recorded, a conversation from a call is gone once you hang up.
- **Text Message** – I love text messages. Quick and to the point. Also, use text when you want to send a photo, directions, or something you want the receiver to have for a long time.
- **Email** – Email is quickly losing steam. Email is good for records and more extended business conversations. When I say records, I mean you can retrieve emails fairly easily, and they are safe, but so many go unread. This is one of the reasons I am not crazy about email newsletters.
- **Notecard** – These are magical. Nothing crazy. Simply a few sentences to check-in and remind your client you are there and always ready to serve. Example:

> Jon–
> Checking in as usual. Hope all is well, and you're enjoying the summer. Real estate is keeping me busy, and I love it. Always here if you need me. Take care.
> Jeff Discher | Broker

- **Face-to-face** – Powerful. Nothing beats face-to-face physical interaction. These are time-consuming but worth it. Get as many of these in with as many different people as possible. Meet out in public for lunch or coffee, and stack your meetings. Plan one after the other in the same venue to build maximum efficiency.

- **Video message** – This is the newest form of communicating on this list. Why not? We can do it with our phone at any time. You can speak directly to the person you are sending it to, they see your emotions, and you can get a lot more emotion in that than in a text.
- **Social media direct messages (DMs)** – These are convenient because everyone is on social media all the time, so there's a great chance they'll see it while at work with their browser opened. or on their phone. This is very popular with the younger crowds and buyers. But, again, it depends on the way your buyer or seller wants to communicate.

> **PRO TIP:** *DO NOT, I repeat, DO NOT let more than three months go by without some type of communication with every single person in your database. This is hazardous to your business. Once agents let more than three months slide by without communicating with someone in their database, the chances of you reaching out ever again drop significantly. It happens to me. It happens to agents I know and coach. I still get that feeling today when I get sidetracked on a big project, and I look up after a couple of months, and my CRM is all red, meaning I haven't met the standard communication timeline I have set in place to reach out to my database. Stay consistent. I get that compliment from clients all the time. "You're like clockwork, Jeff." It feels good. It means they acknowledge my consistency.*

THERE'S POWER IN CONSISTENCY

I've constantly mention the word *consistency* throughout this book because I believe that consistency alone can make or break your success. Consistency in doing the right things get you desirable results, and doing the wrong things consistently gets you undesirable results. People notice consistency.

I have been selling real estate in San Diego for over 18 years as of 2021. I've been in communications with some of the people in my database since then. I've watched single guys buy a condo; a year later, they're engaged and calling me to sell their place to buy a home because they're now married and want to start a family. I help with the sale of the condo and the purchase of that new starter family home. They have three children over the next several years and call me again to say, we need a larger house. I sell that home and help them yet again. Maybe a few years later, I help them sell that home when the market spikes, and they want to buy an even larger home. Yes. I have done that several times. It's an incredible part of my job. That's all because of my communication and consistency over time.

I'm staying in front of my database and providing value to the point that when they thought of real estate, they thought of Jeff Discher. That's what you want. That's what you can do. That's how you set up your career to last for years. The better your relationships, the more consistent the referrals. The more consistent your referrals the less you have to search for "new" business. You can build a steady stream of referrals by and for people you like and want to work with just by being consistent.

ACCEPT CLIENT INVITES

Another activity I strongly encourage is to attend every event your clients, past clients, and members of your database invite you. Birthdays, kids' birthdays, family member birthdays, weddings, dinners, social events, baby showers, networking events, seminars, house warming parties, and any other invitation you receive. This should be a no-brainer. This is also your window of opportunity to be introduced to all their friends as the "realtor." Bring a stack of business cards with you. Don't be tacky either by walking around passing your cards out or dropping them on tables. Wait for someone to ask you about the real estate market and strike up a conversation. When you feel it wrapping up, pull out a business card and offer it to the person you're speaking with to get them to continue their conversation later.

    I've been invited to many events, and I try to attend as many as I can. It's been tougher recently because I'm much busier than I was when I was just selling homes. But it never fails. Every time I walk into a client's event I've been invited to, my client stops the event; introduces me to the crowd; and always says, "This is my REALTOR®. If anyone is looking to buy or sell a home, this is your guy! He's the best." Imagine that! I literally could not pay for better advertising. For the rest of the event, I get to walk around as the REALTOR® and answer a bunch of real estate questions. Yes, it can be annoying. Sometimes you're trying to enjoy yourself and not talk shop, but you are aiming to make six figures in your next twelve months. You can party later. Let's get intentional. Get a client or two. And at a minimum, get a few people to add to your database. It works. DO IT. I encourage all my agents to attend every event that they can. Every event is a networking opportunity and a chance to see your clients and catch up—win-win.

LOST TOUCH, NOW WHAT?

While you were sorting out your database from Chapter 8, there's a good chance you came across people you kept on your list and knew they were going to be a difficult call. You saw their name and got that uncomfortable feeling. We all make mistakes. If you have fallen out of contact with certain people over the years, and now that you're in a new business, real estate, and you want to reconnect, that's ok. Reach out. If that person is really a friend or decent acquaintance, they will be happy to hear from you. Even if there was some turmoil before, be the bigger person and make the call. Call excited to let them know about your new career and encourage a meet-up. Coffee. Beer. Break the ice. Real estate will flow naturally when you start catching up and talking about what each of you is doing.

Let them know about your new endeavor and how you would love to earn their support. Notice I said EARN. That's right. Don't make a call and have a beer and expect a referral. Getting the relationship back on good and current terms was a great start. Now you have to prove your credibility. Now you have to provide value over time to that person, so they learn to trust you and eventually refer you. Again, this comes from doing great work consistently.

> **PRO TIP:** *Before you ask anyone for business, ask them if there's anything you can do for them. Is there any type of client they are looking for in their career or business? How can you help their business or well-being?*

Relationships in life are essential. In every aspect of life. Relationships in business can be the difference between being successful and barely making it.

Another crucial aspect of relationships when it comes to business is understanding your client. How do they think? What do they need and want? What's important to them? How do they make decisions? Imagine if you could get inside your client's head and see the answers to all these questions.

Imagine knowing if your client made decisions based on their gut or data? Do they make decisions fast or slow? Do you need to explain every step and procedure throughout the process, or does your client just want to sign the paperwork and read it later? Do you speak fast or slow to your client? How do you communicate?

Take a look at yourself for a moment from the outside. Step outside of yourself and look back at all your traits, personally and physically, your attitudes, how you handle drama, and situations that don't go your way both personally and professionally? Do you like watching sports on the weekends or going camping? Maybe the beach. Maybe you love running marathons on the weekends. Whatever it is, it's what you like to do. It's tough to find anyone exactly like you in all ways. What happens, though, when you meet someone and find one or two things in common? Does your guard come down a little? When you're talking with someone at a BBQ and realize you both recently saw the same movie. Or you both drive the same truck. Or have the same sense of humor. BOOM. Instant friends. It happens all the time.

A great example is in the movie Step Brothers, when the two brothers first meet and aren't getting along. Then they each ask the other a series of three personal preference questions to which they both say the same answer at the same time. After the last question, one asks look the other, "Did we just become best friends?" and the other one says, "yep"—then they high-five and become best friends. This is a great example of what I'm talking about here. They were at each other's throats, and then the minute they stopped and realized they had common ground, they were best friends. Imagine finding three things in common with a potential client? Would that be powerful? Yes, yes, it would. The key is to recognize those opportunities and connect with not only your current clients but with the potential lines as well.

So what's the best way to do this without knowing the person? We can check out their social media and get a decent sense of what they like and their lifestyle. This is actually a great way to start feeling out your client. See what they like and how they spend their time. This is not to be creepy; this is to understand your client. The better you can understand your clients, the better you can communicate and resolve their problems. You want to find common ground as soon as possible because that's how you start building trust. That's what commonalities do; they connect us.

Have you ever met someone and chatted for a few minutes and felt like you've known them forever. Pay attention next time; you will notice that you probably established common ground right away. It could be a piece of clothing that the other person recognizes or is wearing themselves, it could be you both went to the same school, it could be you both have children that are the same age, it could be that you both drive the same car, to could be you both like to fish, it could be you both like the same football team, it could (You fill in the blank.)

The opposite is also true. You could meet someone several times and still feel uncomfortable around that person. More than likely, you have never found common ground. No connection points. They like red, you like blue. They like baseball, you like basketball. They like country music, you like hip hop. They want to eat an unhealthy choice, you want a healthy choice. It could also be that they like or dislike something you like. Maybe it's a client. Maybe it's a co-worker. It's that person that you just can't seem to connect. It may not even be bad. There's just nothing there. You'd rather spend time with someone else. That's the easy way out, especially if you're trying to build a real estate business. You need to learn to connect with as many people as possible. Eventually, you will be able to pick and choose your clients; for now, let's learn an easy way to connect with everyone.

> **PRO TIP:** *One thing I learned when I was at Keller Williams—and that I still use to this day—is the DISC behavioral assessment.*

This was a game-changer. Try it on yourself first. Don't try to fool it. Just answer the questions. The questions will not make sense at first, but study the profiles and increase your self-awareness. You will be able to use what you learn to improve yourself and your interactions with others. The DiSC is a behavior self-assessment tool that identifies for main personality profiles. There are more in-depth assessments like The Caliper Profile or the Myers-Briggs Type Indicator; however, for simplicity purposes and ease of use, we will stick to the DiSC. The DiSC behavioral assessment is the oldest of the oldest style of personality tests. I like it because it's simple, easy to understand, and easy to apply. The research shows that the most successful real estate agent profiles are high "i's" with "D" as the secondary. This is the preferred profile for all salespeople in general. The "i" is the influencer and with traits such as being outgoing, upbeat, and the life of the party. They talk to everyone and love to network. They do very well in open houses because they talk to everyone and leave a lasting impression. The "D" is the direct, let's get down to business personality that comes out. If you were only a "D," you are not likely to talk to too many people. For example, Steve Jobs was an off-the-chart "D." Now you may be asking, "Jeff, if I'm an 'S' or 'C,' does that mean I can't be successful?" No, not saying that at all. I'm saying that the research shows that the "i-D" combo breeds the most success in sales, especially in real estate sales. It makes sense. These people are outgoing, direct, and have fun doing it. Now your assistants are typically "S's" and "C's." They are organized, cautious, careful, steady, and precise—just what you want. A great partnership would be a rainmaker agent who's an "I-D" and a rockstar assistant who's an "S-C." Boom! A well-moving machine. The funny thing about these combos is each would hate to do the other's job, which is why it works so well.

BUILD LASTING RELATIONSHIPS

Take the free DiSC test at MyDiSCprofile.com.
After you're done come back and take a look at the chart.

After you take the DiSC assessment, study it, and understand the concepts and characteristics of how it works, have someone you know very well take it. However, write down on a piece of paper what you think they are before taking the test based on the chart. (See Appendix H: Using the DiSC Assessment to Up-level Your Business for more on the DiSC assessment and how to use it.)

> **PRO TIP:** *Write down the ten closest people in your life and see if you can identify their DiSC profile. After you have them all written down, send them each the link to take the test. Again, it's free. The people that take it typically agree with the results or at least part of the results. It was a pretty accurate description of me. This is practice for the real world. In the real world, you need to be able to meet someone and identify them much quicker without knowing them, so this exercise helps you practice, which makes perfect.*

Now that you have established your profile, the next step is to identify your client. This is very powerful in a rapport-building way. Imagine if you knew you were working with a high "D" as a client. You would know to be concise and direct. Only give the facts—no small talk. Get me what I want and move out of my way. I have other things to do. This is how it's going down, and it may seem demanding. That's how you would deal with a "D" and build a relationship.

Now, say you were working with a "C" as a client. You would need to be extra patient and explain everything. Maybe even a few times. Start setting the expectations well before you start looking. Educate, educate, educate. You should be educating all your clients no matter what profile, but "C's" just need a little more DiSCussion and explanation. They may stress a little more than others during the home buying process. They may ask for additional information and question everything. They want details. If you were working with an "I," you need to be upbeat and positive. Be ready to have some fun. They may be too much at times but are always the life of the party. When they buy, they buy fast. If you were working with an "S," they would need extra care. They typically need hand-holding. If you come in raging, they will run. Speak slowly and thoroughly. Continue to reassure them everything will be ok.

You can find books and articles written on DiSC and videos on the Internet. I highly recommend you learn how to profile for the sake of communication and frustration. It works. If you come at a client the wrong way, it would be the last way. (For more on DiSC, see Appendix H: Using the DiSC Assessment to Up-level Your Business.)

3 ACTION STEPS

1. Contact five people in your database and enter your conversation in the database.
2. Use your three pillars and database to find three things in common with a person before you go to meet the potential client.
3. Take the DiSC assessment and learn to identify the profiles of your clients and vendors.

CHAPTER 11

BUSINESS PLANNING

If You Fail to Plan, You Plan to Fail

If you fail to plan, you are planning to fail. This is true on so many levels, but especially true in business. Imagine traveling across the USA with no map. Even worse, imagine not having a destination. You would waste a lot of gas, time, and money and be very frustrated. At some point, you may even give up. It doesn't sound like a trip many of us would want to take. Yet, that's what you are doing by starting a real estate career without a business plan. Every year that goes by without you having a business plan in place is time you spend spinning your wheels and going hundreds of miles in the wrong direction. I learned this lesson the hard way, so please listen carefully. Each year in real estate is basically a start over. If you don't have a business plan, you will have no direction. You will never know if you are making progress or on track to improving and moving towards your goals. A well-defined business plan outlines all aspects of your real estate career for the year. You can have daily

"If you fail to plan, you are planning to fail."

— BENJAMIN FRANKLIN

goals, weekly goals, monthly goals, quarterly goals, yearly goals, five-year goals, and even ten-year goals. These will all be different but should all tie together.

For a real estate agent, your business plan is the What? Why? When? Where? And Who? Any areas in which you want to set goals, you need to have a plan for how you will get there. The business plan is directly related to your goals. The goal is the destination; the plan is the map to get here. You set your goals and tie that to a plan that will help you accomplish them. (For details on what you need to include in your business plan, see Appendix J: Creating Your Business Plan.)

For example, if you want to make $1M dollars in gross commission in real estate sales, you want to know how much you would need to sell to reach that goal. Each plan should be unique to each goal. If you want to sell twenty-five homes in a year, determine how many sales per month that would take, what action is needed to make that many sales, how many calls, how many face-to-face meetings that would take to achieve, and how many conversations to the same person or entries in the database? How much would you have to spend, what type of client you would need, where you would need to meet this person, and so on. If it takes you one hundred calls to make one sale, you would need to make 3,000 calls to reach your goal. You can do that for every goal and every situation. If you are starting from scratch, you will need to estimate and adjust as you go. As a start, track how many calls it takes you to make a sale, how many open houses it takes you to make a sale, how many face-to-face meetings it takes you to make a sale, how many intentional social media posts it takes to make a sale, and any other activities you add to your plan. Do this for three months to get a good idea.

Each city will be different in terms of what will be needed to make six figures. You need to consider the average home prices you will be selling in your primary market, the commission splits you will be receiving from your brokerage or team, and the cost of overhead to keep your business running at its best. You can do this anywhere if you follow the steps I have outlined for you in this book. You can be successful with discipline, consistency, and hard work.

3 ACTION STEPS

1. Write your business plan.
2. Identify the weekly, monthly, and yearly goals needed for you to meet the vision you set out in your business plan.
3. Run the data for your local market. How many sales at the average home price will it take for you to make your goals a reality?

CHAPTER 12

YOUR VENDOR TEAM

Choose Your Team Wisely

Who makes up your vendor team, you ask? Great question; these are all the people you will work with to get the real estate transaction completed. When you first start your real estate career, you will receive calls upon calls from various vendors, all trying to convince you to work with them.

It's a conversation I have to have with my new agents on day one. For years I've been saying: the real estate process, whether buying or selling, starts with the real estate agent. The real estate agent is the one out on the streets and marketing to get the potential home buyers or sellers. Once we get the client, we distribute them to all our vendors. It's very unlikely that a vendor will send you a deal. Nine out of ten times, it will be you, the agent originating the deal, and you passing it along to all the necessary vendors. So, what does that mean? It means we have the power. We get to choose the

"Teamwork divides the task and multiplies the success."

— AUTHOR UNKNOWN

people to whom we refer our clients. We get to set up and select the team that we want to help us complete the transaction.

What exactly is a vendor? A vendor is anyone that will help facilitate the transaction and is necessary to complete the transaction. Here is a basic list:

- **Home Loan Lender** – This person is responsible for your client's home loan. They are a significant part of the transaction. The lender is the first or second person the home buyer will meet during the process. They will take all the necessary paperwork and data to qualify your client for the home loan. They collect data associated with credit reports, income, debt, and employment. The lender is the gatekeeper to the home loan process. Choosing the one or two lenders to work with is essential and can make or break your deal. Choose wisely. Meet with a few lenders and discuss your business plan and your goals to make sure you are on the same page.

    If you work twelve-hour days and weekends, make sure your lender works the same schedule. If you are looking to only work with first-time home buyers, make sure your lender is experienced and likes to work with first-time home buyers. If you are working with military buyers, make sure your lender is a Veterans Affairs (VA) specialist. If you are working in the luxury market, make sure your lender knows jumbo loans. Make sure you also get along with your lender. I've been working in the real estate market for eighteen years, and I've been with the same lender since day one. We get along, and it makes it easier to get deals done. Ask questions. A lot of questions. Choose wisely.
- **Title Insurance Representative** – Title insurance is insurance for the title of your home. The seller's agent typically chooses who will issue the title insurance policy for the transaction.

How does it work? When a home is sold, before the title can transfer to the new owner, the title must be clear. What does a clear title mean? It means the title is free and clear from all encumbrances—such as a lien—that can be attached to the title of the home.

There are four common types of liens that can be attached to a property due to an owner's outstanding debt: a mortgage lien, mechanic's lien, tax lien, and a judgment lien. For example, if the seller had work done on the home and didn't pay the contractor for the work, the contractor can attach a mechanic's lien to the title. And before a home seller can transfer the title to the new buyer, there must be no liens in place; all outstanding debts must be paid.

So why do you need title insurance? You need it so you are then able to obtain a clear title from the title company and so you can confirm that the seller and owner information on the title actually matches the seller's information. And per California real estate law, it is mandatory. (The rules and regulations for a clear title may differ from state to state. To confirm any requirements for your area, check the local real estate law.)

Now, if six months later a plumber comes out of the woodwork and says the new buyer owes $14,000 from an old plumbing bill that the previous owner didn't pay, who's responsible for that $14,000? Could you imagine calling your buyer and telling them they are responsible for the previous owner's debt? Wouldn't that be fun! This is when the title insurance comes to the rescue. Because the title company missed that discrepancy with the plumber's lien, it would be responsible for paying that debt. That's why it's "insurance."

The title insurance company is ensuring that the title is clear, so it would be their responsibility to pay the debt. That's why this part of the puzzle is very important.

YOUR VENDOR TEAM

Make sure you have a reputable and trusted title representative on your side. Again, meet with a few to get a feel for how they do business and make sure you both have the same business sense and plans in mind. Title representatives need to work for your business. They can help you grow your business and should. We basically hand them their business so ask for their help. Make all your representatives work for your business. There are a lot ways they can help you. Meet with a few reps and ask what they do for their REALTORS®, and most importantly, make sure you get along with them.

- **Escrow Company** – Escrow is another vendor that is typically chosen by the seller's agent. What and why is escrow important? Escrow is the third-party accommodator that guides the transaction and holds it all together while crossing the t's and dotting the i's. They collect all data points in the transactions, clarify them, organize them, and ensure everything is executed per contract.

Again, make sure the escrow company and officer work your exact schedule and be available when you need them. This is very important. My team and I work crazy and long hours, and we need a team that works like we do. You don't want to ever feel like your bothering your vendor team. Escrow doesn't work weekends, but the right one will work for you. Real estate is a 24/7 business, so when people in the industry tell me they don't work weekends, I get hesitant and concerned. A majority of real estate transactions happen on the weekend. Escrow controls the closing, documentation preparation, dealing directly with the buyer's bank and the seller's bank, the profit disbursements, commissions, and for everyone, including YOU getting paid. If you want to get paid, make sure you work with a reputable escrow officer that you like. Escrow companies typically have sales representatives as well. These are employees of the title company that go office to office and check-in on the agents working with their company. They can also help grow your business by helping out in different ways.

- **Home Warranty** – The home warranty vendor is also chosen by the seller. The most important thing about choosing your home warranty representative is making sure their home warranty is reputable and services their clients. I've seen nightmares in this department. Not all home warranties are created the same. Like anything, some are good, and some are bad. Ask around. Meet with a few representatives to determine who you like and check their credentials and reviews to ensure they properly service their warranties.
- **Wood Destroying Pests Inspection** – Also known as termites, can be a real problem, and for some loans and contracts, it becomes necessary. What do they do? They make sure your home is free from termites, dry rot, and any wood-destroying pests. First, the vendor will do an inspection, and based on if they find termites or not, they create a report and document any issues found while doing their inspection. Once the inspection is completed, the repair work is to be done before the close of escrow.

    There are instances when the work is paid for through escrow but not performed until after due to timelines. Again, this can make or break a deal, so make sure you go with a reputable company that works on your schedule. Depending on how severe the work is, termite damage can be a major health and safety issue. Again, find a reputable company; they're out there, find one.
- **Home Inspector** – This is a big one and is chosen by the buyer and buyer's agent. The condition of your home is very important and should not be taken lightly. Once you remove your inspections and repair contingency, that's it. If anything happens after you close, it's on your clients. What does the mean? It means that you should hire a qualified inspector that has an excellent reputation. In my career, I've seen them all. There are inspectors

YOUR VENDOR TEAM

that don't want to make the agent mad or blow a deal, so they are conservative when calling out repairs. Please remember, your client's interests come before yours. Always in all ways. This is not the inspector you want.

There's also the other side of the spectrum, the inspector that calls out and makes a big deal out of every minor issue. That is also a sure way to blow a deal for no reason. Finding one in the middle is vital. An inspector who calls out everything and knows how to explain it to the buyer in the right way. Every home will have deferred maintenance and normal wear and tear. Don't lose a home for a client because there are scuffs on the baseboards or the smoke alarms have dead batteries. Yes, this happens. Your home inspector can make or break a deal, so make sure you choose the right one that works well with you.

3 ACTION STEPS

1. Make a list of all the vendors you will need. (See list above)
2. Ask other agents that you respect and trust who they include in their vendor team. Create a list of referrals from each vendor category and set up interviews.
3. Choose your vendor team and meet with each of them to strategize ways they can help you grow your business.

SUMMARY

If you want a successful and extraordinary career, you must set up your office and environment to win. You have the skills you need to win the mental game, and build a solid foundation for your business; now it's time to reach that next level of success through intentional investments in your business.

Now investment means several things: you are investing your time, energy, and money into becoming better and attaining more. The right tools can accelerate and organize your business, making it a lot more efficient and with less stress. It's better to start with as much in place as you can swing than to wait until it's a necessity.

When you start to scale, you must be organized and efficient. Never stop striving for the newest tools, technology, and apps to make your business run smoother. Stay in front of your clients better. Stay ahead of the curve.

Please remember, you don't need every tool available. Just because a tool or process works for someone else doesn't mean it will or has to work for you. Speak with other agents and brokers and discuss what they are utilizing and why. How is it working for them? Most experienced agents will tell you all about their trials and tribulations. Pay attention, listen, and learn.

Implement as many of the tools listed below as you will use:

Real Estate license (REQUIRED) – You can get your license with an investment of three months and about $500. That's the easy part. The real work starts once you actually begin working for a broker.

Smartphone – This is your direct line to your clients, the Internet, your calendar, your database, your camera, the applications you will be using every day to build your business.

Laptop/Tablet – Although most tasks can be handled by your phone, you will also need a laptop, tablet, or both, when it comes time to draw up a contract or read one in its entirety. The tablet helps when it comes to marketing and editing since the larger screen is convenient for the fingers and easier on the eyes.

Customer Relationship Manager (CRM) – Software that acts as the single source for all of your client information and communication. Some newer agents can't afford a CRM initially and have horror stories of losing deals and clients because they failed to follow-up because they had no system in place.

Multiple Listing Service (MLS) – The MLS allows brokers to see one another's listings of properties for sale with the goal of connecting homebuyers to sellers. This is the base for real estate professionals looking for properties for their clients or posting a new property for sale. You must be licensed and pay the yearly membership dues and fees to be part of the MLS.

The most important tool as a real estate professional and the one you want to prioritize purchasing is your CRM. Remember when I said you need to invest time and energy in addition to money? Building relationships is the place to channel all of the resources you have available to you.

The hardest part about real estate is generating a client. Getting a lead. A referral. Basically, waiting for a real person that trusts you enough to allow you to help them find or sell a home. It's the largest transaction of an individual's life, and you have to have to command a deep level of respect and competency for someone to let you lead them through that process.

A study conducted by the National Association of REALTORS® asked home sellers why they didn't use the REALTOR® who originally helped them buy their current home to sell their home, and the number one answer is that they couldn't remember who it was.

Please invest the time and energy in your clients to do an amazing job through the sale and beyond. Be consistent in how you show up for your clients and your contacts. I have been selling real estate in San Diego for over eighteen years as of 2021. Since then, I've been in communications with some of the people in my database, and my business has boomed because of it.

I have helped the single guy purchase his first condo and then years later move to a house in the suburbs with his new wife. They had three children over the next several years and called me again to say, they needed a larger house. I sold that home and purchase a new larger home. Then when the market spiked, I helped them sell their home and buy an even larger home. The better your relationships, the more consistent the referrals. The more consistent your referrals, the less you have to search for "new" business. You can build a steady stream of referrals by and for people you like.

Focus on the goals you will need to set to reach your first six figures. You need to consider the average home prices you will be selling in your primary market, the commission splits you will be receiving from your brokerage or team, and the cost of overhead to keep your business running at its best. You can do this anywhere if you follow the steps I have outlined for you in this book. You can be successful with discipline, consistency, and hard work.

Investing resources in your clients and business plan is a solid beginning; the next step will set you up for long-term sustained growth. Your relationship with your CRM is intentional, and your relationship with team vendors should be just as intentional. These are the people you will rely on to make sure that the transaction goes smoothly. You will want to make a list of all of the vendors you will need and select vendors who will support your business growth goals.

CONCLUSION

YOUR NEXT MOVE AS A REAL ESTATE AGENT

Join a Team or Work Solo?

Should I join a team or go out on my own? This is a question I get when newer agents ask my advice before, or right as they're getting their license. Should I join a team or be on my own? This is a great question with a lot of support for both sides. Teams have recently become very popular in the real estate profession. When I first started back in 2004, most agents were on their own. If you were successful, you had an assistant. The team of 2021 is a different beast. It takes a special dynamic, and when you get it right, it really works. If the person leading isn't ready to lead, the team will experience inefficiency and frustration.

Let me start by giving you a brief story of how I started Discher Group, one of the top producing teams in beautiful San Diego, California. As I've mentioned, I've been a licensed real estate agent

> "It is literally true that you can succeed best and quickest by helping others to succeed."
>
> – NAPOLEON HILL

since March 2004. I started my career relatively aggressively, earning Rookie of the Year my first year and making just over $100,000 in commissions. In my second year, I almost doubled my previous year and made $184,000. Having the high ambitions I do, I decided to get my broker's license in 2006. I opened my first office in 2007 and closed in 2008 due to the market crash of 2008. If you lived through it, you know it wasn't pretty. Thousands of people lost their homes and everything they had, including myself.

The crash had no mercy. The real estate market was rocked. The short sales and foreclosures were everywhere you looked. I had several properties and lost most of them. I had a couple agents, and they didn't produce because I didn't know how to lead, train, or transition to this new distressed market. I remember getting the call in August 2008 from my lender who was in panic, letting me know that half of my pipeline was dead. He started naming off file names, saying their loans were dead, and they didn't qualify anymore. The banks had changed their guidelines overnight and were not grandfathering any loans. I had clients with U-hauls packed, ready to close and move into their new home, and I had to tell them they didn't qualify anymore and that they couldn't purchase a home. It was a difficult time and one from which I never thought I'd recover.

When I started my first brokerage firm, I just wanted more. I felt like the only next step was to get my broker's license and open my own office. Even though I had a brokerage and others to look out for, I was still in no position to lead myself—let alone a team. It's one of the mistakes I see many newer and experienced agents make.

They have success for two or three years, get a little recognition, and decide to start a team. You see this in a lot of professions. A person does well in a profession and wants to go out on their own and start their own business. What happens? A high percentage fail.

Why? They were good at what they did, but they didn't know how to run a business. It's different. The same happens in real estate. Agents get a few good years under their belts and think they're ready to start a team. It took me thirteen years of experience, a broker's license, seven real estate designations, hundreds of homes sold, training several rookies over the years, reading more books than most, listening to hundreds of hours of the most respected business leaders, attending several seminars, and studying the greats before I agreed to start another team.

I wanted to make sure I was capable of taking another person's career and livelihood into my hands. That's essentially what you're doing by starting a team. You are saying you understand real estate sales, marketing, leadership, and contracts enough to train people to do the same and become successful at it. That takes a specific type of individual, a person who can put others before himself or herself—someone with a "We" before "Me" mentality. This is no easy task and requires major self-awareness. It's a mindset shift—a paradigm change. You must become obsessed with bringing out the best in people and having paramount patience. The leader's job is to keep the team ahead of the curve. Keep up with the latest trends, marketing tactics, and market activity while serving their clients. Be there when the team needs you, no matter what. Continually improve your skills by becoming a lifelong learner in leadership and real estate. Always improving yourself and your business 1 percent better every day in every way.

I don't have kids, but I could imagine it's like having a kid in a sense. A team is actually like having many kids, and I don't mean that negatively or condescendingly. I like the analogy of raising a baby from infant to first grade; that's getting a new agent freshly licensed. There will be a lot of frustration on both ends. The job as the leader/parent is to make sure you always support them, looking out for their well-being as they learn this new world and navigate through the process. If you do your job correctly as a leader, that agent grows into their business with the right habits and disciplines, and the agent succeeds. It takes both the agent and the leader working together and believing in each other to make it work and to truly bring out the best in each other. Authentic leadership is one of the hardest things I have ever done. It challenges so many of my beliefs when it comes to people's success. I always thought I could just tell someone what and how to become successful, and they would listen, execute, and succeed. I know what I'm telling them works; I've witnessed it work for so many people. They just needed to listen and execute. I learned quickly that's not the case. For some people, that works, and for some, it does not. For most, it does not. People are on their own timelines and learn and progress at different rates. Some start to succeed right away, and some take months. The faster you can learn the person, the faster you can learn how to train them.

A friend of mine and team leader from Keller Williams in San Diego, Stephen Jack, and I were having a similar conversation. I explained how some of my agents get it, listen, and take off while others seem stuck and frustrated. He said something I'll never forget. I had an instant paradigm shift. He said, "You can hire and train a bunch of people like yourself, Jeff and build a tribe, or you can learn to hire and train everyone and build a legacy."

That statement was very powerful and profound for me. I realized at that moment I had another major challenge on my hands. I really needed to learn about people, not just business. What makes them tick? What motivates them? What's the fastest way to get this person to understand the business and really connect? Why do some people learn one way and some learn another?

People are people, and business is business. A real leader must constantly work on becoming the best at both. It takes both. I say this because if you decide to join a team, you need to make sure the leader will help you succeed. Ask agents on the team what they like and don't like about the team. What activities are the team's focus? Is the team driven and focused on culture or production? Technology-driven? Laidback or high energy? Is there formal training, mentorship, leads, a formal office, or do you work from home? Are there standard hours the team operates together? Are there team meetings, and what do they cover? What type of business planning do they offer? Do I have direct access to my team leader at all times? These are all questions you want to ask the team and yourself.

I have been giving the same advice for years now when asked this question. My answer is always the same, join a team and become a buyer's agent or assistant. Again, make sure you like how the team runs and operates its business, and most importantly, make sure you LOVE the culture. Culture always wins. You will be surrounded by people just like you and with the same goal. You will have a leader who typically has had sales success in his or her career and is now teaching otters how to fish.

Ask if you can attend a team meeting a few times to understand how the team operates and to get a sense of the day-to-day energy. When bringing new agents to the Discher Group, I ask them to attend two or three team meetings before scheduling the interview. It saves a lot of time and frustration because they get to be on the team for a few weeks without actually being on the team. Prior to implementing this hiring process, I would hire people I liked, then run them through the entire onboarding process only to realize eight weeks later that they were not a good fit. Everyone gets excited when they come to the office and interview, then when it's time to do the work, the excuses come, the limiting beliefs kick in, and it's not pretty.

You will grow so much as an agent if you join the right team. They will push you to be the best version of yourself and show you a higher level of success than you could achieve by just going through the motions. Real estate agents change teams every few

> "Every action you take is a vote for the type of person you wish to become."
>
> — JAMES CLEAR

years because they didn't take the time in the beginning to find the right fit for the working style. As you invest in your personal development, make sure to check-in with your mentors to ensure you are on the right path.

You have what it takes to be a real estate agent who earns six figures in the next twelve months. I know you do because I just spent the last twelve chapters breaking down precisely what you need to do to make this happen. The average real estate agent will not complete more than four transactions in a year, but I have good news for you. You didn't come here to be average.

At the end of the day, numbers don't lie, and your production will be a direct output of your habits. Make your client's needs your priority, and you will do well. Les Brown said it best, "Help others achieve their dreams, and you will achieve yours." Your dream of becoming a real estate agent who generates six figures or more a year is possible if you remember the simple steps to take care of the needs of your clients.

BOOM.

APPENDICES

APPENDIX A

STAGES OF A SUCCESSFUL CAREER

The content in Appendix A is also referenced in Chapter 1: Morning Ritual—Set Up Your Day to WIN.

YOUR PATH TO SUCCESS

I am excited to give you the tools you need to become a successful real estate professional. The industry will always have room for talented and driven individuals. You are probably already asking yourself if all of these strategies and concepts will work in real life. I have good news—I know that they work because these are the exact stages I went through in 2004, and I see my newer agents working through them now.

These stages are essential in guiding you into a successful career. Of course, over time, your gut check will become stronger, but while you build up those muscles, these written stages will keep you moving forward and give you confidence in the knowledge that you aren't alone. These stages are discussed in more detail in Chapter 1: Morning Ritual—Set Up Your Day to WIN and are also offered here in an abbreviated version for quick reference.

Stage 1: Pre-Licensed or Freshly Licensed Real Estate Agent. Getting your real estate license costs a few hundred dollars, and anyone can pass the test. You also realize that every brokerage is willing to offer you a job. You think you've made it and the good life is ahead, but at this stage you are extremely naive.

Stage 2: First Week of Life as a Real Estate Agent. You're still excited but confused and frustrated. There's no clear plan. There are a bunch of different strategies and tactics everyone says you should use to get clients. This first week is when you start to realize how it works, and it's not what you thought.

Stage 3: A Few Months into Life as a Real Estate Agent. Excitement has started to fade at this point and turns into deeper frustration. You begin blaming everyone for why you're not succeeding. This stage is where most people quit or start to fall into financial trouble. This can be the breaking point for most, but this is when you need to double down. Right before you feel like nothing is going your way, **KEEP GOING.**

Stage 4: First Client and Escrow. You keep pursuing relentlessly and pick up your first client, help him get approved, work for a couple weeks searching for the perfect home, and BOOM! you're in escrow. Your excitement shows, and people start to see your confidence. You've made it! Or have you just begun?

Stage 5: Plateau. Your phone stops ringing. The referrals have stopped. This is another quitting point for most newer agents. They stopped following the schedule that got them to this point, and they basically have to start all over again at Stage 3.

Stage 6: Two Years in. At this point in your career, you understand the game. You have the discipline and habits in place as a base to continue to crush your goals. Your goal should be to minimize those ebbs and flows and keep a steady stream of business by sticking to the schedule. It's not easy, but it is simple.

Stage 7: Repeat the process. As you repeat the process, you learn to master your schedule, time blocking, and lead generating activities. You may also decide to hire an assistant or a showing specialist, or you may start a team.

APPENDIX B

WRITE DOWN YOUR GOALS

The content in Appendix B is also referenced in Chapter 1: Morning Ritual—Set Up Your Day to WIN.

This is an image of the actual goals I literally wrote down every single day during 2020.

And as I indicated in chapter 1, one of the habits I created for myself is to write my goals and affirmations, and I encourage my team members, trainees, and coaches to use the S.M.A.R.T. (specific, measurable, achievable, relevant, and timely) goal writing system for their own goals. See the following S.M.A.R.T. goals writing chart below for directions on how to write and execute your goals.

Specific	• Your goal should be clear and detailed and should explain exactly what you are going to do and how.
Measurable	• Your goal should be measurable. A tangible measure will help determine how successful you were with your goal.
Achievable	• Your goal must be achievable and help motivate you to suceed. Impossible goals will only demotivate you.
Relevant	• Your goal must coincide with your overall objective and fit in with the bigger picture.
Timely	• Your goal should have a set timeline with specific start and end dates so your goal is set in stone and set to be delivered.

You want to consider the full lifestyle you envision for yourself, not just your professional career. What do you want to accomplish six months from now? A year? Five years? Write your goals (and affirmations) that will help you make this week successful so you can achieve your full potential over the long-term.

APPENDIX C

READERS ARE LEADERS

The content in Appendix C is also referenced in Chapter 1: Morning Ritual—Set Up Your Day to WIN.

The smartest people I know are readers. Hell, the most successful people I know are readers. This is across industries. I'm not saying you MUST read to become successful; I'm saying it increases your chances by a lot. Set a goal for yourself to read a certain number of pages a day. If you don't read or haven't read for a while, start small with around five pages per day. It will be tough. It will demand patience and focus. Like a muscle, the ability to focus becomes better over time. You build on it. Before you know it, you're reading thirty to fifty pages per day, every day.

I finished reading Tara Westover's *Educated* in two days. It's a 330-page book, and I am a busy guy. What does this tell you? It tells you it's very good—the type you can't put down. To me, this book represents how we have shaped much of our lives based on those we are closest to and look up to, mostly our parents and family. We go through life never questioning our belief systems because why would we dare question the people we care most about. We would never want to hurt their feelings.

The truth is we believe them whether they're good, bad, or both. Humans rarely break the mold. We limit our own possibilities by adhering to this mindset. Learning to separate ourselves and think on our own as early as possible is the key. I challenge you to question everything you've ever believed in life, money, business, religion, health, relationships, and even your regular thoughts. It's challenging. I know. The truth is it's powerful.

Reading and experiencing *Educated* may have intrigued me enough to write my own memoir.

You may not be able to finish reading 330 pages in a single week (and I *did* read; I did not listen to the audio version) but you can increase the number of pages you read every day. It's very addictive because you see the benefits and the difference in your conversations and understanding. It becomes something you look forward to. You will find yourself buying more books than you can read. I have stacks of books around my house and office that I still need to read. Actually, there's a Japanese term for owning more books than you can read–*Tsundoku*.

You can bulk up your number of pages by using audio apps like Audible, 12 Minutes, Kindle, Apple Books, Blankest, or whichever you prefer to help you get in additional knowledge while you're driving, exercising, traveling, or any other activity that allows.

Here is a list of books I recommend for business and life:

1. *The 10X Rule: The Only Difference Between Success and Failure* by Grant Cardone

2. *Atomic Habits: An Easy & Proven Way to Build Good Habits & Break Bad Ones* by James Clear
3. *The Compound Effect: Jumpstart Your Income, Your Life, Your Success* by Darren Hardy
4. *Focus: The Hidden Driver of Success* by Daniel Goleman
5. *How to Win Friends & Influence People: The Only Book You Need to Lead You to Success* by Dale Carnagie
6. *How to Work a Room: The Ultimate Guide to Making Lasting Connections In Person and Online* by Susan Roane
7. *Jab, Jab, Jab, Right Hook: How to Tell Your Story in a Noisy Social World* by Gary Vaynerchuk
8. *The Magic of Thinking Big* by David J. Schwartz, Ph.D.
9. *Maximum Achievement: Strategies and Skills that Will Unlock Your Hidden Powers to Succeed* by Brian Tracy
10. *Mindset: The New Psychology of Success* by Carol S. Dweck, Ph.D.
11. *MONEY Master the Game: 7 Simple Steps to Financial Freedom* by Tony Robbins
12. *The One Thing: The Surprisingly Simple Truth Behind Extraordinary Results* by Gary Keller
13. *Rich Dad, Poor Dad: What the Rich Teach Their Kids About Money that the Poor and Middle Class Do Not!* by Robert T. Kiyosaki
14. *The Science of Success: The Secret to Getting What You Want* by Wallace D. Wattles
15. *Shoe Dog: A Memoir by the Creator of Nike* by Phil Knight
16. *Start With Why: How Great Leaders Inspire Everyone to Take Action* by Simon Sinek
17. *Think and Grow Rich* by Napoleon Hill
18. *Total Money Makeover: A Proven Plan for Financial Fitness* by Dave Ramsey
19. *Traction: Get a Grip on Your Business* by Gino Wickman
20. *What to Say When You Talk to Yourself* by Shad Helmstetter, Ph.D.

21. *Your Next Five Moves: Master the Art of Business Strategy* by Patrick Bet-David

There you go! There's your start. I can assure you that if you read every single one of these books, you will have some great new ideas, a lot of AHA moments, and will eventually get paid more—that's what you're looking to do. This is your starting point. After you read the books on the list I provided, keep going. Make it a habit to be a lifelong learner. You will notice the changes. People will notice the changes. Get READY!

APPENDIX D

HABITS CAN BE GOOD OR BAD

The content in Appendix D is also referenced in Chapter 2: Discipline and Habits—Show Me Your Habits, and I'll Show You Your Future.

A habit is something we condition ourselves to do and, over time, that we learn to do without conscious thought. You brush your teeth every morning and night because your parents taught you to develop that habit as a child. If you are a runner, you have a habit of running at a specific time each day for a set number of miles. If you tell yourself that you are too busy to cook, then you are likely in the habit of ordering food that is not good for your body.

Successful people have better habits than most. When I say "better," I mean better in terms of moving one step closer to becoming the best version of themselves. They have learned that the better are one's habits, the more successful one can become and the easier it is to achieve goals.

HABITS CAN BE GOOD OR BAD

Anyone can develop better habits—just as is the case with the habit of drinking coffee aids in developing a tired person into a perky person. Developing a better habit is a matter of changing the habit loop.

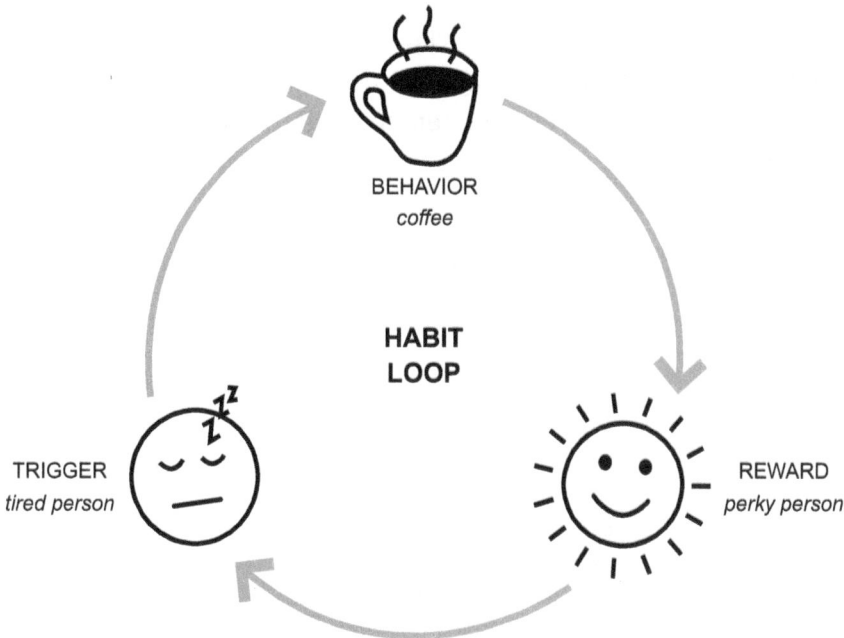

Your trigger (cue) is the cause of your craving or your desire to complete a behavior (response) and get your result (reward). Here is a simple formula for forming good habits,

CUE	CRAVING	RESPONSE	REWARD
1	2	3	4

TIME ⟶

In the example of being tired, you may be in the habit of reaching for a cup of coffee, which then results in increased energy.

The trick here is to change either the trigger or the reward to keep your habits in line with your goals.

For example, one of my goals is to increase my endurance. Each night before I go to sleep, I lay out my workout clothes so that when I wake up (trigger), I see my workout clothes (cue), and I crave working out so that I feel good and increase my endurance (reward). Focus on increasing your desired behaviors so that this time next year you are closer to embodying the person you want to become.

APPENDIX E

DESIGNATIONS HELP YOU PROVE YOUR VALUE

The content in Appendix E is also referenced in Chapter 3: Personal Development—Improve Every Day in Every Way and Growth and Chapter 4: Time Management and Time Blocking—That Which Gets Measured Gets Done.

Do you know the difference between you and the hundreds of other real estate professionals in your city? It's what you know. Designations are a way for you to prove your value before you ever open your mouth. They are additional certifications you can acquire by attending either an online course or classroom course, passing the test, and paying the fees and costs associated with the designation. The costs run between two hundred dollars and $4000 per designation. Some require multiple classes to receive one designation. Here is a recommended list of designations to get you started:

1. Accredited Buyer's Representative (ABR)
2. Accredited Land Consultants (ALC)
3. At Home with Diversity (AHWD)
4. Certified Commercial Investment Member (CCIM)
5. Certified International Property Specialist (CIPS)
6. Certified Negotiation Expert (CNE)
7. Certified Real Estate Brokerage Manager (CRB)
8. Certified Residential Specialist (CRS)
9. Counselors of Real Estate (CRE)
10. e-PRO certification
11. Graduate, REALTOR® Institute
12. Master Certified Negotiation Expert (MCNE)
13. National Association of REALTORS® Green
14. Performance Management Network (PMN)
15. REALTOR Association Certified Executive (RCE)
16. Residential Accredited Appraiser (RAA)
17. Resort and Second-Home Property Specialist (RSPS)
18. Seniors Real Estate Specialists (SRES)
19. Short Sales and Foreclosure Resource (SFR)
20. Society of Industrial and Office REALTORS® (SIOR)

As of this printing, the above designations are the ones offered. The list may change, so please do your own research to identify the ones that best fit and interest you and your business. Visit https://www.nar.realtor/education/designations-and-certifications or the National Association of REALTORS® website to see the latest information.

APPENDIX F

MANAGE YOUR WEEK TO WIN THE YEAR

The content in Appendix F is also referenced in Chapter 4: Time Management and Time Blocking—That Which Gets Measured Gets Done.

The most successful real estate agents have timing down to a science. They manage their time down to the minute and have a calendar, an assistant, a structured schedule, or an internal clock they have mastered. I use some of all these methods, but the biggest piece I rely on is my weekly calendar. I know what I am supposed to be doing each day, every day. Below is an example of my weekly schedule:

Weekly Schedule Planner

Time	Sunday	Monday	Tuesday	Wednesday	Thursday	Friday	Saturday
7:00 a.m.		GYM SESSION					
7:30 a.m.							
8:00 a.m.		READ BOOK AND WRITE GOALS					
8:30 a.m.							
9:00 a.m.		LEAD GENERATION FOLLOW UP					
9:30 a.m.							
10:00 a.m.							
10:30 a.m.							
11:00 a.m.							
11:30 a.m.							
12:00 p.m.		LUNCHTIME					
12:30 p.m.							
01:00 p.m.	OPEN HOUSE	CONTENT CREATION DISTRIBUTION					OPEN HOUSE
01:30 p.m.							
02:00 p.m.							
02:30 p.m.							
03:00 p.m.							
03:30 p.m.							
04:00 p.m.		OPEN HOUSE					
04:30 p.m.							
05:00 p.m.							
05:30 p.m.							
06:00 p.m.							
06:30 p.m.							
07:00 p.m.							
07:30 p.m.							
08:00 p.m.							
08:30 p.m.							
09:00 p.m.							
09:30 p.m.							
10:00 p.m.							

Your calendar can get more detailed than this; use it as an example for context and as a starting point.

Time management and time blocking are so necessary while working to get to six figures and beyond because once you get a few sales going, it's very easy to get caught up babysitting the deal to make sure it closes. This is one of the biggest mistakes an agent can make. I see this mistake hindering careers and holding people back from having breakthroughs. What do I mean? I mean that when you don't time block, creating space on your calendar that is consistently dedicated to engaging specific activities that will drive your success, it's easy to forget to do the activities that you did to get you the deals you currently have. Set up time blocks in your online calendar or print it out and post it somewhere you can always see it. Program yourself for success by following a set schedule and sticking to it no matter what.

APPENDIX G

LEVERAGE ACCOUNTABILITY TO BECOME SUCCESSFUL FASTER

The content in Appendix G is also referenced in Chapter 4: Time Management and Time Blocking—That Which Gets Measured Gets Done.

No man or woman becomes successful in a vacuum—you can't do this all alone. Use accountability to increase your level of success and take action on your grand plans. Personal accountability is the most likely to fail so instead of counting on yourself to do the right thing every time, build in public accountability such as scheduling open houses and promoting via video on social media.

At Discher Group, we use the following weekly accountability form. Feel free to use this as-is or create your own. Either way, implement some type of accountability form.

LEVERAGE ACCOUNTABILITY TO BECOME SUCCESSFUL FASTER

Weekly Production Goals   Monthly Sales Goal _____ # of Units _____

Phone Contacts/Text Messages | Week of _____ / _____

1. _____ 2. _____ 3. _____ 4. _____ 5. _____
6. _____ 7. _____ 8. _____ 9. _____ 10. _____
11. _____ 12. _____ 13. _____ 14. _____ 15. _____
16. _____ 17. _____ 18. _____ 19. _____ 20. _____
21. _____ 22. _____ 23. _____ 24. _____ 25. _____
26. _____ 27. _____ 28. _____ 29. _____ 30. _____
31. _____ 32. _____ 33. _____ 34. _____ 35. _____
36. _____ 37. _____ 38. _____ 39. _____ 40. _____
41. _____ 42. _____ 43. _____ 44. _____ 45. _____
46. _____ 47. _____ 48. _____ 49. _____ 50. _____

Note Cards

1. _____ 2. _____ 3. _____ 4. _____ 5. _____
6. _____ 7. _____ 8. _____ 9. _____ 10. _____

Social Media Video Messages

1. _____ 2. _____ 3. _____ 4. _____ 5. _____
6. _____ 7. _____ 8. _____ 9. _____ 10. _____

Face-2-Face Meetings

1. _____ 2. _____ 3. _____ 4. _____ 5. _____

Business Card hand outs

1. _____ 2. _____ 3. _____ 4. _____ 5. _____

New Added People to Data Base

1. _____ 2. _____ 3. _____ 4. _____ 5. _____

APPENDIX H

USING THE DISC ASSESSMENT TO UP-LEVEL YOUR BUSINESS

The content in Appendix H is also referenced in Chapter 5: Focus Points of Business—Go All-In on Three Activities and Chapter 10: Building Lasting Relationships—Create Clients for Life.

Reference the DiSC Profile Chart and the different profile breakdowns. Notice the characteristics of each profile and how they may operate or think differently. Are there people in your life who you can identify by any or some of these characteristics? Are you able to identify yourself by any of these characteristics?

USING THE DISC ASSESSMENT TO UP-LEVEL YOUR BUSINESS

Dominant
- Direct
- Decisive
- Doer
- - - - - - - - - - - - -
- Domineering
- Demanding

Task Focus

Compliant
- Cautious
- Careful
- Conscientious
- - - - - - - - - - - - -
- Calculating
- Condescending

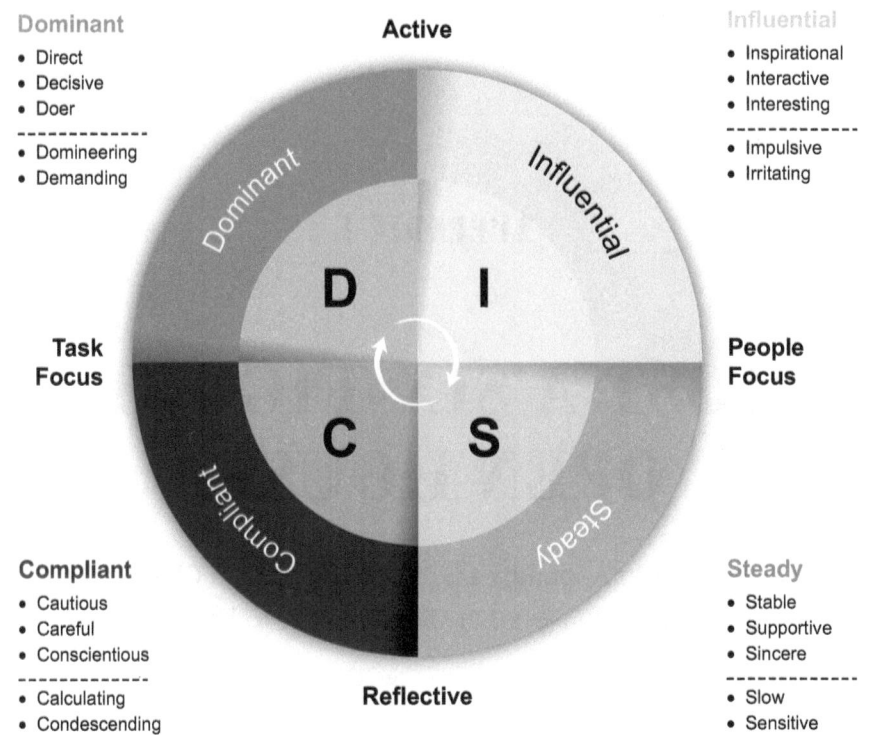

Active

Reflective

Influential
- Inspirational
- Interactive
- Interesting
- - - - - - - - - - - - -
- Impulsive
- Irritating

People Focus

Steady
- Stable
- Supportive
- Sincere
- - - - - - - - - - - - -
- Slow
- Sensitive

APPENDIX I

HOST A SIX-FIGURE OPEN HOUSE

The content in Appendix I is also referenced in Chapter 7: Open Houses—Let Clients Come to You.

When it comes to presentation, here is a list of items you will need. Some of you are saying, "Jeff, I can't afford all of that right now." I get it. Start with what you can, then build on it. The company or team you join will more than likely give you your first six open house signs. Your goal should be to have twenty. I'm not joking. You want to stand out. **STAND OUT!** Don't be shy. You want to make six figures, right?

SIX-FIGURE OPEN HOUSE PACKAGE

- Have, at a minimum, ten open house directional signs. The **MORE**, the **BETTER**. (I used to put out twenty to thirty signs.) Make sure they are clean, clear, and understandable.

- Flags with poles on your signs equate to a small **INVESTMENT** with big **RESULTS.**
- Put balloons on your signs when possible. (These are just flags on steroids.)
- Map out the busiest intersection and stop signs in the area to decide where to place your signs.
- Get a folding table with a custom, fitted cover bearing team or company branding. (This is a small cost compared to the level of professionalism attained. These table covers are between $150 and $300, and the table is around forty dollars.)
- Create posts for all social media channels promoting your open house and ask your audience to share.
- Have custom flyers designed. The average agent is lazy and will just print out the multiple listing service (MLS). By having better production value and information they can't get elsewhere, you will make a positive lasting impression. The goal is to be remembered in a professional way.
- In this book, I've given you all the apps you need to perform everything I've asked you to do. Set up templates for "open houses," "just listed," "just sold," "offer accepted," and "for sale." Google "real estate flyers" for ideas. The design apps have a slight learning curve when you first start, but you'll get used to it in no time. **BEWARE:** *It can be very addicting, so monitor how much time you spend on these things and outsource the work as you can afford it.*
- Have your laptop out and open with the front wrapped with your information. You can get this at skinit.com. You can also get a phone case branded for your business as well. It costs less than one hundred dollars for both and is well worth it. You can also sit at coffee shops with your laptop open, facing the patrons and traffic for brand exposure. Two agents on my team, Ben Biggs and Maxwell Ventura, both got their first clients from coffee shops doing just what I said. It works. Do it.

- Have small giveaways for visitors as a way for them to remember you. We bring branded pens, notepads to take notes, water bottles, key chains, shirts, and workout towels.
- Burn scented candles—nothing with too overbearing of a fragrance; have a candle with a scent that is clean and welcoming.

HOW TO FIND OPEN HOUSES EMAIL/TEXT MESSAGE TEMPLATE

Melissa,

John Smith here. I'm a real estate agent with ABC Realty. I want to congratulate you on the beautiful listing at 123 Broadway in La Mesa. It's a great property. I wanted to let you know I am willing to help you sell it by holding open houses every day until it sells. You wouldn't need to do anything. I will do the necessary research on the property and be as prepared as possible for any questions potential buyers may have about the property.

Here's what to expect from me if you allow me to hold open your property:

- Market the property on all social media platforms before and during all open houses.
- Continue to market the property on all social media until it sells.
- Place flyers at the one hundred homes closest to the property.
- Set up a minimum of ten directional open house signs with flags or balloons.
- Get to the property early and open all window treatments.
- Turn on all the lights before the open house begins and turn off all lights and lock up at the end of the open house.
- Each day after the open house, I will email you an activity report detailing how many people showed up to the open house, who showed any interest, and who had comments—whether good or bad.
- Alert you of any potential offers that may be coming our way.

My goal is to personally bring you a buyer and showcase your listing in the best possible way.

As soon as you give me the okay, I will get started with my preparations for the open house.

Thank you for your time.

Professionally,
John Smith | REALTOR® | ABR | GRI | RENE | SRES
ABC Realty

What do you think? If you received this email, how would you respond? There's a good chance if you weren't available to hold an open house, this may be the next best thing. Imagine after the agent holding the open house sends the listing agent the activity report as promised in the email detailing the number of parties that attended, any interest, comments, and potential offers; the listing agent can forward all the information to the seller. It's great information to use as an indicator of whether the home is priced too low, too high, or just right. The comments are great as well because they give direct buyer feedback. This can be important when it comes to price adjustments and repairs.

APPENDIX J

CREATING YOUR BUSINESS PLAN

The content in Appendix J is also referenced in Chapter 11: Business Planning—If You Fail to Plan, You Plan to Fail.

Referrals and consistent communication with your database are awesome, but the next significant investment in your business is the time you spend on your business plan. Some of the basic information you should include in your business plan is as follows:

- Number of closed transactions based on the average price of the homes you sell
- Marketing plan for the year and what it entails
- Marketing budget for the year and where each dollar is allotted
- The number of appointments you must go on each day, each month, and each year to reach your goal
- The number of calls you must make each day, each week, and each year to reach your goals

ABOUT THE AUTHOR

Jeff Discher has been making highlights despite his incredibly challenging upbringing, coming out of hardships and achieving so much in his career, that it was worthwhile for him to write a book. His achievements and skills acquired just through his real estate career—let alone through all the other areas of his life—are remarkable. A dedicated real estate broker for more than eighteen years, having a team of high achieving real estate agents, and mentoring people to become the best versions of themselves are a few of his motivators that make Jeff jump out of bed each morning. Being an inspiration for people who want to achieve greatness in their lives and for those who want to create a positive change, Discher shares his reflections and advice in *6 Figures in 12 Months*. He has been featured by Yahoo, *San Diego Reader*, and *The San Diego Union-Tribune* and has had his own show on ESPN Radio, featuring topics focused on health, wealth, and real estate. He has grown a respectable audience across most social media platforms, always providing progressive value through his content. His goal and mission are to inspire as many people as possible to not only crush it in real estate but to help everyone become the best versions of themselves.

www.ingramcontent.com/pod-product-compliance
Lightning Source LLC
Chambersburg PA
CBHW020754230426
43673CB00022B/442/J